LET THERE BE LOVE

LET THERE BE LOVE

Themes from the Bible

edited by

Kris Tuberty

THE THOMAS MORE PRESS
Chicago, Illinois

The material in this book appeared previously, in different form, in the newsletter *Markings*, published by the Thomas More Association.

ISBN 0-88347-241-4

CONTRIBUTORS

Kathleen Cannon
James A. Connor
Andrew Costello
Henry Fehrenbacher
Timothy Fitzgerald
Sean Freeman
Norbert Gaughan
Andrew M. Greeley
Marcella Hermesdorf
William Herr
Mary Peter McGinty
Rawley Myers
Daniel E. Pilarczyk
Paul J. Wadell

Contents

BLESSING FOR THE INCREASE OF LOVE

May the Spirit's warmth renew the love of your life
May God's strength help you to be brave
In tenderness, not weak in petty strife
May God's wisdom your sensitivity save
When frustration and discontent are rife
So that gently passion's bond be remade
May your delicacy be keen as a knife
And your gentle persistence never fade
Till love's old romance is at last remade
And may the God of love bless you and
Bind you together as he binds the universe
With the attraction of gravity's power
Father, Son and Holy Spirit

by Andrew Greeley

NO GREATER LOVE

by Sean Freeman

THE greatest sacrifice of all is being called upon to lay down our life for another—or others. There is no greater love than to do this voluntarily, the scriptures tell us, and both fact and fiction provide scores of examples: the person in a lifeboat who quietly slips over the side in the night so that the dwindling supply of rations will go further; the soldier who throws himself on a live hand grenade to absorb the lethal blast in a crowd; the mother who perishes while shielding her baby from burning or freezing. That is love indeed.

The story of God's testing of Abraham's faith is powerful and even shocking. For us, who have heard it many times, the shock value is diminished because we know that it turns out all right—God relents at the last second. But it is still not totally in accord with everyone's idea of how an all-loving God should treat one of his children. It is a cruel test by human standards, the sort of grim practical joke that we might hesitate to inflict on our worst enemy.

No matter how many children Abraham might have had, it would still be a terrible thing to ask that he take any one of them out to be killed by his own hand and then made into a burnt offering. But Issac was an only child, conceived and born when Abraham and his wife, Sarah, were in their nineties, long after they had given up hope of having any children at all, so the demand was especially harsh.

In fact, it was more than harsh—it must have seemed to Abraham like the cruelest of ironies. For God had told him that not only would he and Sarah have a child but that he was to name the child Isaac and through this child there would exist a covenant between God and Abraham which would endure for all ages and result in the birth of a whole people. Abraham found this both so wonderful and at the same time so incredible that, Genesis tells us, he actually rolled about on the floor laughing.

Then, having kept his word and given him Isaac as promised, a scant few years later God not only decides to take Isaac back in bloody fashion but to break his covenant, as well. If ever there was reason to resent, reject, and perhaps even curse God, Abraham had one.

But he did none of these things. He did precisely as God told him to do. Scripture records not the slightest hesitation or grumble of dissent on his part. Nor is there any reason to suppose that Abraham felt God was bluffing. The God that Abraham knew, and which the Old Testament repeatedly shows us, was not a God who had to bluff. If he said don't eat the fruit of this one particular tree, he really meant it. If he said he would send a great flood to destroy the wicked, that's precisely what he did.

No, Abraham went out to sacrifice Isaac without the slightest hope of reprieve. To Abraham, God's ways were not those of humankind, perhaps, but they were not to be questioned. Isaac had been a gift from God and if God wanted him back—so be it.

Taken quite literally, the story of Abraham and Isaac teaches the lesson that faith—true faith—in God must be unquestioning and absolutely constant. Whether God chooses to relent—as he did in this case—or not, as often happens in the tragic situations of life, he is still God, our God, and his ways are not to be questioned.

In a figurative sense the story shows that we are completely in God's hands, but that those hands can be merciful. By extension into the New Testament, however, it shows dramatically just how great God's love for us really is. He sent his only son freely into the world to suffer for us and redeem us. But, unlike Isaac, he would not be spared. He was indeed made into a living sacrifice offered on our behalf. He died so that we might live in God.

And it is in just this context that Paul tells us we simply have no grounds for fear about the ultimate outcome of our lives. God has proven in the most convincing way possible that he hears us. "Since God did not spare his own Son," he writes, "but gave him up to benefit us all, we may be certain, after such a gift, that he will not refuse us anything he can give." If we have been saved through such a sacrifice of love, then who can accuse us or judge us? Not even Jesus himself. "No," says Paul. "He not only died for us—he rose from the dead, and there at God's right hand he stands and pleads for us."

Through Abraham's faith God kept his covenant with

him. Through the sacrifice of love which Jesus made—in complete faith and fidelity with his own Father's will—God keeps his covenant with us for all eternity.

Greater love than this there simply is not.

Not all sacrifices, thank goodness, are of the magnitude which Abraham and Jesus were asked to make. But all of us are called upon to make some sacrifices in life—not just the sort which circumstances mandate, and over which we have no control—illness, handicaps, death or separation from a loved one. There are sacrifices which we can make either out of love or for some greater good, or simply refuse. These generally involve passing up something good, or putting ourselves into situations of extra work and trouble, perhaps even into an awkward or embarrassing situation for the sake of someone else's good or betterment. Parents who forego luxuries and often real necessities for their children's education are but a single example. The man or woman who could rightfully take all the credit for something at work, but chooses to remain silent so that others may share in the glory is another. The point is that any sacrifice of ego, ease, comfort, even material possessions made freely on behalf of another mirrors in some small way the love which radiates from the great sacrifices—unto death—which the scriptures tell us God values so highly as proof of our unshakable faith. They are a very powerful form of the sort of silent prayer which seeks no righteous justification or reward and which Jesus extols as the most effective and pleasing in the sight of God.

THIS IS MY BELOVED SON

by Andrew Greeley

SOME people are magic. They have a mysterious combination of psychological and physical attributes that make them instantly attractive. They walk into a room and every head turns in their direction, and everyone pauses to listen. They leave and everyone experiences a feeling of disappointment. They make a suggestion or a request and everyone rushes to comply. Whatever this mysterious "star quality" is, it is more than mere physical good looks, more than intelligence, more than personality; it is a mixture, a blend, a combination of what we call charm, elegance, or grace.

The heavenly father, we know from the Gospel, was deeply in love with Jesus. Jesus' charm, his attractiveness, his grace has captivated and captured God's pleasure. Every child is appealing to his parent, indeed, intensely appealing. In the gospel it is asserted that the appeal of Jesus to his heavenly father is in some sense not unlike the appealing attractiveness, charm, gracefulness that an earthly child finds in its parents' eyes. A parent looks at a child and sees himself, his flesh and bone, his blood, his genes, his personality, and in this reflection he sees some of his personal gracefulness. Similarly, God looks at Jesus and sees himself reflected. He is attracted by his own grace as it is revealed and manifested in his son Jesus.

Formerly, many of the definitions of "sanctifying grace," which may have been precise and accurate theologically, didn't seem to mean too much. We could define sanctifying grace if we had to, we could even assert that it existed in our soul; but we had no feel for what it was and no sense of its importance other than that we knew we lost it if we committed mortal sin and couldn't get into heaven without it. The Gospel, however, gives us some idea of what sanctifying grace is. It is what God saw in Jesus that made him say: "This is my beloved son in whom I am well pleased." Jesus was a reflection of God's own goodness and "grace," that is to say, his appeal, attractiveness, charm, elegance, which exist in Jesus in a superabundant way. They also exist in each of us. To say that we "have" sanctifying grace is to say that God's goodness and love is in us, and when God looks on us he sees his love reflected in us and he is intensely attracted to us.

God is more attracted by the reflection of his selfhood in our "grace-fullness" than two lovers are attracted by the image of themselves as beloved, which they see in each other. The intensity, the passion, the almost obsessive concentration between two lovers is a mild emotion compared to the attractiveness God finds in us and that he sees reflecting his grace.

It must be emphasized that our basic gracefulness comes from the very fact of our existence and is rooted in our fundamental nature as creatures made in the image and likeness of God. This gracefulness can never be lost. It can, of course, be dampened when we turn away from him in sin, and the grace which Jesus brought into the world can restore us to full favor with God. But that full favor restored is a gift that could not be possible without the basic favor, the basic appeal, the basic fact that our very nature is Grace. God can save us as he did Jesus (with a difference but also a similarity). "This is my beloved child in whom I am well pleased." He can say that about us even when we are caught up and imprisoned by sin, and he can say it with special vigor when we have accepted his ever-present forgiveness of our sins and our sinfulness.

Most of us are not fantastically good looking. We all get old and lose the transient attractiveness of youth. We have fears, inhibitions; our personalities are not much more appealing than that of a dead stick much of the time. We are either afraid that if we don't make a lot of noise and say something outrageous, people will not notice our existence and in fact we will not exist, or that we are not worth noticing, not worthy of saying anything. Either way we feel irrelevant, unimportant, nothing. That God could say of us, as he said of Jesus, "This is my beloved child in whom I am well pleased" is astonishing. We are full of grace because God loves us. That is what grace is—God's love reflected in us.

There will come a time when the warmth of God's love will ignite the grace inside us and we will become the flourishing, flowering, dazzling person we were designed to be. That will come in God's own time. But even in this world, if we believe we are graceful, full of grace, we will begin to glow more brightly than we did before, and people will notice us not because we are afraid we will cease to exist but because it is no longer possible to hide our personal splendor, our own dazzling grace, our own reflecting of God's love behind fear, anxiety, and irrelevance.

LET IN THE LIGHT OF LOVE

by Daniel E. Pilarczyk

ONE of the great characters in fiction is Ebenezer Scrooge. At Christmas time we all like to hear again the story of this "squeezing, wrenching, grasping, scraping, clutching, covetous old sinner," who is "secret, self-contained, and solitary as an oyster." Dickens writes about Scrooge's meanness to his clerk Tom Cratchit, to his nephew Fred, to the gentlemen who were collecting money for the poor. In the night visions which follow the appearance of Marley's ghost, Scrooge is led through his own past, through the present, through the future, until he sees himself for what he is: an unloving old man who offers no good to anyone. By the end of the visions Scrooge realizes that he must change, and he does. He buys the prize turkey for the Cratchits, offers a big donation for the poor, and makes up with his nephew. He becomes a new man "who knew how to keep Christmas well, if any man possessed that knowledge."

But there is another facet of Scrooge's story—a Lenten facet—which is important for our reflections today. Scrooge's problem wasn't just that he no longer loved anybody. It was also that he no longer let anyone love him. His conversion required a change of heart. He isn't made

Themes from the Bible

whole and healthy again until he accepts the warmth and hospitality of his nephew's family and allows himself to be regarded as a second father by Tiny Tim. Accepting love, allowing ourselves to be loved, is as much a part of the agenda of a good life as is loving.

In the Gospel, John writes of the conversation between Jesus and Nicodemus. Nicodemus had come to Jesus out of the night to discover what he was all about. Jesus tells him, and he also tells us. The Son of Man is here because God loves this human world of his and wants to give it eternal life. And those who do not attain eternal life remain in the darkness, not because they haven't done enough to deserve the light, but because they have simply refused to accept the light and the life that God offers in Jesus.

Our problem is that we instinctively believe that there is no such thing as a "free lunch." We are suspicous of what seems to come too easily. Whether it's the offer of a free six-month magazine subscription or the offer of a friendship or the offer of eternal life from God, we tend to turn gifts down if they look too good. There are quite a few reasons for this.

One is that we are afraid of hidden obligations. We are afraid that we will be suckered into something and then, when it's too late, we will find out that we owe more than the something is worth, that more is expected of us than we really want to pay.

Another reason is that we are convinced that we can't really have anything unless we have worked for it. If we work for it and earn it, then it's really and truly ours. Nobody can take it away from us. What we personally achieve is the only thing that we can hang on to, the only thing that is really ours, the only thing that is really safe.

But the third reason why we are suspicious of what comes too easily is the most deeply rooted of all. We suspect the "free gift" because we know that we don't deserve it. Deep in our heart is a conviction, based partly on original sin and partly on our own life experience, that we are not really lovable, and if someone wants to be nice to us, it's because that somebody doesn't really know us. We are reluctant to accept another's gift because we are afraid that the giver will eventually find out who and what we really are and take the gift back again.

When it comes to accepting the offer of God's love for us, these reasons for holding back are simply absurd. When God extends his arms to us and says, "Come and live with me," our reasons for hesitating just don't make any sense. "I can't afford what it costs." Of course we can't afford what it costs, because it's not for sale. "I don't want anything I haven't worked for." In that case, we might as well just stop living right now, because our very life and everything we have in life is already God's gift. "I don't deserve it." Obviously we don't deserve it. God doesn't expect us to. In fact, the one thing God asks from us is to admit that we don't deserve his gifts, and then to accept them anyway. God is bigger than our human hangups and failures and sins, and to try to make God subject to the same dynamics that we use in our ordinary life is to try to cut him down to our own human size. It is to love darkness rather than light.

Learning to let God love us, learning to open our secret,

self-contained, solitary hearts to the Lord's presence is a lifetime job. But there are a couple of things we can do to be sure that we are at least facing in the right direction.

One is to make use of the sacrament of Reconciliation. "Already, obligations," somebody will say. "We knew that there was a hidden price somewhere in here!" Not really. The sacrament of Reconciliation, going to confession, is one of God's gifts to us. It is our opportunity to acknowledge that we aren't all we should be, that we really don't deserve God's love, but then to hear him say, through his priest, "I know, but I love you anyhow. And you need to hear from me, your Lord, personally and individually, that my love for you is greater than anything you can do to reject it."

Another way in which we can stay in touch with God's love, another way in which we can open our hearts a little wider, is to try to modify our perspective a bit. It's hard to believe God's love for us if we look at life through the eyes of an unregenerate Scrooge, if all we see is bad. But try looking a little harder for God's love in your life and see what happens. Remind yourself when you get up in the morning that God's love has brought you to the beginning of this day, and that no matter how grim the prospect of the day may be, he is powerful and loving enough to spend it with you. When nice things happen, don't presume that they are merely a prelude to catastrophe. They are little love notes from the Lord. And when the going gets tough, remember that the power of God's love in your life doesn't depend on how much you do for him, but on how much you are willing to let him do for you.

24

TO KNOW HIM IS TO LOVE HIM

by Rawley J. Myers

THERE are many stories of successful failures. One is told by the philosopher Herbert Thomas Schwartz. When he was a youth he wished with all his heart to be a great pianist. He dreamed about being honored and idealized on the concert stage. But the more he tried the more he failed. He says, "I think this frustration was the beginning of God's grace for me." In the end he had to admit that he would never be above average. This humiliation made him humbly return to studying philosophy. He says now, "I shudder to think what would have happened had I succeeded in music." He would have been an unbearable pompous prig, he says. His failure, which so crushed him in his young years, was a blessing for which today he says, "Thank God!"

In everyone's life there is confusion. We often want what God does not want, and vice versa. Sometimes we must suffer, like the philosopher, before we come to find out what is best for us. Suffering, to be sure, has a purpose.

Life can be very confusing, and today there is a good deal of confusion in religion. People are mixed up; they do not seem to realize that Christianity is to know Christ. This is the purpose of our earthly existence. If we fail in

25

Themes from the Bible

this, we fail altogether. If we succeed in everything else, popularity, prestige, making money, pursuing pleasure, and yet do not know Jesus, our life is a failure. As Christ said, "What does it profit a man to gain the whole world and lose his own immortal soul?" It was indeed these words, often spoken by Ignatius Loyola, that brought the brilliant and popular University of Paris professor Francis Xavier to Christ.

In Westminster Abby, the historic London church, there are many statues, most portraying men once famous but now scarcely known. Fame is fleeting, popularity is ephemeral. Better to be a failure and find God.

In the epistle to Corinthians, Paul speaks of being "called by God." We are all called by God to know Christ, so that we can love him and follow him. We can hardly be true Christians, Christ-followers, if we do not know him. To know Jesus is to love him, and then it is not a burden but a joy to do as he wishes. Parents enjoy doing things for their family; they anticipate their needs. Why? Because they love their children. If we really knew Christ and therefore loved him, we wouldn't say, "I hate to do that" but, rather, "Let me do more."

Frank Sheed entitled one of his books *To Know Christ Jesus*. This is the heart of our faith. A person can gain eternal life without knowing a lot of Catholic trivia—how many candles for benediction, the names of the vestments worn at Mass—but a Christian cannot enter heaven without knowing Christ.

Some Christians think they know Christ, but do they? If they really knew Christ, would they turn religion into

LET THERE BE LOVE

a discussion club and the parish into a debating society? Is this what Christ wants? Jesus told us that deeds, not words, are what please him. One can almost hear him say, "I am sick of all your words—I want you to do something to help those who are in need, not just talk about it all the time."

Youths indeed seem to see things at times more clearly than do adults. They say they are tired of us telling them about Christianity—they want to see it. And until they see it, they turn off our many sermonettes. As Ralph Waldo Emerson said, "I cannot hear what you say because what you do thunders so loudly in my ears."

Youths love Mother Teresa of Calcutta because she talks little but shows beautifully what it means to follow Christ.

The young are not taken by pious platitudes, especially those by people who do not practice what they preach. One who is all in tears preaching about the poverty of Christ but who himself lives in material splendor is hardly going to get his message across, least of all to the young who hate phonies.

Teens are looking for Christ. They want to see him. If we preach Christ, they have a right to see him in us. Do they? Do we proclaim in our daily lives his otherworldly philosophy? Teens are like Mohandas Gandhi. Once a Christian was telling him about Christianity. Afterwards he, a Hindu, said, "It is a beautiful teaching—I wish sometime I could see a Christian." His irony was not lost on the speaker. G.K. Chesterton said, "Christianity has not been tried and found wanting, it has never been truly tried." Is this the case with us? Are we whole-hearted or

Themes from the Bible

half-hearted Christians? Someone said that the worst advertisements for Christianity are Christians. Is the gentleness of Christ and his kindness to be seen in us, or are we hostile individuals like our unbelieving neighbors? If we do not show Christ in our daily dealings, can we say that we know him?

John the Baptist confessed he did not know Christ at first. It is easy for any of us to be confused about him. It takes a good deal of prayer to know Jesus well. And too many these days are too busy to pray. They are full of good intentions, but never get around to it.

Not a few Catholics in our times have walked out on Christ. It is easy to walk out on him if a person does not know him; it is impossible to desert Christ if one really knows him. Some, unfortunately, have childish notions about Jesus, gained from the pretty pictures and little stories learned in First Communion class. But these notions do not hold up in an adult world, and pretty soon these people drop out of religion. What a pity! People turning their back on their dearest friend.

The prophet Isaiah says, "The Lord said to me: you are my servant." this is the role of the genuine Christian, like Francis of Assisi. We come to this dying life naked and ignorant. How then can some humans become so pompous, like strutting peacocks? All we have, all we are, is from God, who has been lavish in giving us our countless gifts.

God gave us our greatest gift, his Son, to guide us through the wilderness of life. He knows what little lost children we are. Unless we know and follow Jesus, the fabric of our faith unravels.

LET THERE BE LOVE

Christ taught us that one has no right to expect love without giving love. This is the heart of our religion. We are to be giving people, just as Jesus was. It is in giving love that we grow in love. As Francis of Assisi said, "It is in giving that we receive."

The poverty of the homeless Jesus mocked the wealth of the worldly. His humility showed the foolishness of the proud. He said, "Blessed are the poor in spirit; they are my true friends." Jesus taught that the rich can be poor. A person can have all the money in the world and yet have a heart that is loveless. The worst poverty is emptiness of soul. The teachings of Christ sparkle and flash like sunbeams on a lake. Only the thoughtless say Christianity is dull. It bores them because they do not know Christ. In religion they don't want to think, they only want to be entertained.

Jesus has a passionate desire to draw all people to his Sacred Heart. He greatly wishes us to stir up our hearts and respond to his invitation of love. We must put aside our selfishness and put on the unselfish love of Jesus. We are weak, but if we are humble Christ will help us. He calls to the lowly and enriches them. The ways of grace are many and mysterious, but Jesus, as we see in the Gospels, has a penchant for drawing the insignificant to himself. Poor, struggling, praying souls are his favorites. Christ hides in humble hearts.

LOVE OVER HATE, LIFE OVER DEATH

by Kathleen Cannon

RECENTLY a good friend related to me an experience he had almost twenty years ago that made a profound impression on him. At an interracial workshop in the late sixties, he met a young man who was spending his first year after his college graduation working in Arkansas registering Blacks to vote. It was, of course, a time of bitter racial tension and violence in the South. My friend asked the young graduate whether he had ever experienced any hostility in this dangerous work. The man said that he had and recounted times when he had been beaten and kicked and spit on. "Why didn't you fight back?" my friend asked. "At first I did," the man replied. "And then I realized that the violence has to end somewhere. It has to die with me or it will go on and on."

Occasionally our lives are touched by people whose lives are striking witness of Jesus' teaching in the Gospel.

> They who love their life must lose it . . . If anyone serves me, they must follow me.

These words, the last public words of Jesus, given as a response to those who come and ask to see him, are not merely the communication of an abstract truth. No, Jesus speaks of what he has learned from accepting the conditions of human life, from giving himself to the human project. He knows through experience that the law of nature is the law of human life: death is the way to life; self-emptying the way to fulfillment.

Jesus knows. He knows the world. He knows what rejection and betrayal are. He knows the malice of the human heart—and he alone forgave the woman caught in adultery. He knows the suffering of death—and he cried when Lazarus died. He knows the world in its joys and pains, in its beauty and mediocrity. And he loved the world until the end—until the extreme consequences. Jesus knows, then, and he loves. He died precisely because he made himself vulnerable to the hurt that comes in choosing to relate to others in love.

Jesus is ready to suffer for those he loves because he knows the Father. He knows the one he calls "Abba" as a loving and tender parent who does not issue commands but speaks to the deepest recesses of the heart, who has no conditions on love and forgiveness and whose deepest concern is for his children, especially those most in need (Jeremiah 31:31-34). Jesus came to know and to believe in the love the Father had for him—he learned to do so in the school of suffering (Hebrews 5:8). His human heart is troubled by the prospect of death (John 12:27), and he prays "aloud and in silent tears to the one who had power to save him from death" (Hebrews 5:7). But believing that God would not forsake him even in this, Jesus hands his life over in absolute trust to the Father's love and wisdom.

Themes from the Bible

This is his obedience. By abandoning himself to this love, Jesus comes to the greatest realization of his creaturehood and of freedom. For God rescued him—not by saving him from death, but in God's own way. God gave final endorsement to Jesus' life by saying: "You may be. You may live."

Because Jesus remained faithful, obedient, and loving even in the face of suffering, we are established in a new relationship with God (Jeremiah 31:31). Jesus' handing over of his life in love is not a mere pattern to be followed, a good example. It is, rather, grace bestowed upon us eternally so that the humiliation of the cross can become for us a life-giving mystery in which the one who assumed our humanity enables us to imitate the divinity of his love. He is the source of eternal salvation for all who look at the cross and see God's love for the lowliest.

When we celebrate the Eucharist we do what Jesus did. We commit ourselves to dialogue with those who are far from us; we feel responsible for the people somehow entrusted to us in our family, in school, at work. We forgive those who harmed us, or are even likely to do so in the future. We accept the "worldly experience" of suffering and death, spiritual or physical, not with resignation, but with a loving, hopeful attitude of trust in the Father. And the suffering that is accepted in faith and love becomes, by the power of the Holy Spirit in our hearts, the seed of Resurrection.

To do what Jesus did means to serve and care for others. To serve even when not understood; to serve when we are forgotten. To serve even if this leads to a cross. "If anyone would serve me, they must follow me." We need not go out of our way to look for suffering in a world that is bleeding. But each of us, in large and small ways, must learn to live like that young man, letting hate die in our bodies so that what enters the world as death will return to the world as life. Moreover, we must learn to stand on the side of love and justice and peace, and that will bring its own suffering.

We need to be reminded that believing in God does not shield us from pain and difficulty. Salvation does not mean that God rescues us from what is upsetting or frightening or painful, but that God is with us in anything that life can bring. God's power is never equated with force—even against those who would crucify Christ—but with the disarming appearance of love in this world. In Jesus' life and death we know that we are radically loved and embraced by God. Even in the midst of what seems to be absurdity, there is God. For God is the power of goodness over evil, the triumph of love over hatred, the victory of life over death.

A LEAP OF LOVE

by Andrew Greeley

ONCE upon a time there was a little boy who didn't believe in anything at all that he couldn't see for himself. People told the little boy that the world was round, but as far as he was concerned it was flat. He couldn't see the curvature and he never traveled around the world and, he said to his family and friends, what difference does it make whether it's round or flat? It doesn't affect my life. He didn't believe in the existence of New Zealand because he'd never been to New Zealand, and he thought it was a funny name anyway. He didn't believe he ever had a grandmother or grandfather because all of his grandparents were dead. Nor did he believe in his Aunt Erika who lived in Seattle, Washington, because he'd never seen her. In fact, he didn't believe in Seattle, Washington, because he'd never been there. What difference does it make in my life, he said, whether there is an Aunt Erika or not, whether there is a Seattle or not? Then Aunt Erika sent him a Christmas present. Then he said, all right, he guessed there had to be an Aunt Erika.

He really didn't believe in Abraham Lincoln or George Washington or Douglas MacArthur or even Dwight D. Eisenhower. They were people in picture books but he'd never met them or seen them on television. He believed in Ronald Reagan because he'd seen Ronald Reagan on television and, of course, he believed in Jim McMahon and Otis Wilson and Wilbur Marshall because he'd seen them on television. In fact, he believed in everybody he saw on television.

Now we all would say that this little boy is pretty crazy because if the only people we believe in are people we see personally or see on television, and if the only places that we believe in are places that we've seen ourselves, and if the only scientific observations we believe are the ones we make ourselves, then we really aren't much better than our ancestors who lived millions of years ago. We are prisoners of our own narrow, provincial, parochial world. (By the way, our young friend also thought that the sun revolved around the earth, and when he was told that the earth revolved around the sun, he asked the usual question: "What difference does it make?")

And did I tell you the little boy's name was Thomas?

The point of the story is that even in a scientific age— or one might say *especially* in a scientific age—we routinely take all kinds of things on faith. We believe in general what we read in the history books, what we see on television, what our parents teach us, what everybody with common sense seems to believe, what the teachers in school say. Our belief is a kind of shorthand. We can't verify everything ourselves so we are inclined to take the word of people we trust or who at least have no reason to lie to us. Generally this pragmatic faith is pretty reasonable. Moreover, reasonable or not, it's the only way we can live. The alternative pursued by our little friend Tommy is to live in a world of complete skepticism and cynicism, a world where we can barely find our way through the darkness.

Now faith in the existence of God, faith in God's love, faith in the Resurrection of Jesus, faith in our own resurrection is not quite the same as this ordinary human faith which is essential to our everyday human life. But it's not altogether different either. Basically, in the absence of truth, we tend to believe those who we think are trustworthy, who have no reason to lie to us and, especially, those whom we love. As a matter of fact, faith and love are really different aspects of the same reality. If we admire and respect and revere someone and then find ourselves loving that person, it is very difficult to remain skeptical about what the person says. We are converted into belief in that person, not so much by reasoned arguments, not even necessarily by signs and wonders, but rather because we love the person and we know that the person will not deceive us.

The psychological truth—that faith follows love and that the best argument in favor of the truth of what someone says is that lovability—helps us to understand what went on in the Gospel story of Thomas. While he may have been fond of his fellow apostles, the intensity of his affection for them was not strong enough to constrain his faith. And when Jesus appeared, the exercise of touching his wounds was an irrelevancy, for he saw the one he loved and that loved one was still very much alive. Thomas was ready not only to believe that Jesus was alive but to believe everything Jesus said about the loving Father in heaven.

LET THERE BE LOVE

He was, in fact, rather like his young namesake, Tommy the skeptic, who was perfectly prepared to accept the existence of Aunt Erika after, in an act of love, she sent him a present. The manifestation of love, in other words, constrains us to believe what the loving person says.

When we talk about faith, let us not make the mistake of thinking we are dealing with a rational and intellectual problem, that questions of faith and unbelief can be answered by arguments. The most an argument can do is clear away obstacles to faith. Faith itself is finally a great leap of trust and love on which we not only accept the truth that is offered to us but the lovability of the one who offers the truth. This also we'll not forget—particularly in times of doubt and difficulty and unrest and suffering and loss—that to reject faith, to say there is nothing to believe in, is also a leap of the character and of the personality. For the evidence finally is inconclusive: God may love us or he may not love us. Love may animate the universe or it may not. To accept or to reject love both require a leap of the personality, one into hope and the other into despair.

Tommy in our story says it doesn't make any difference whether he believes in New Zealand or Seattle. Whether the earth is round doesn't affect his life one way or another. But Tommy will find as he grows up that he really has to trust other human beings and that it does make an enormous difference in life. In order to survive and to live, humans have to make a leap one way or another. Either into faith and trust in which we become open and loving persons or into cynicism, unbelief, and despair, in which case we become closed, rigid, and narrow persons. More-

37

over, saying that we believe, saying that we trust in God's love and in the message of Jesus, is not enough. As we all know, there are many who profess belief but who are in fact narrow, rigid, cynical, unbelieving people, and some who in their heads are not sure what they believe but in their lives are indeed men and women of faith.

Doubt and faith are not absolute contradictions, but rather polarities between which we oscillate. Thomas, the doubting apostle, is a classic example of the oscillation of faith. He both believed and did not believe and then, finally, in the revelation of Jesus, he believed. But still it seems safe to assume that as life went on, Thomas, like all of us, still had troubles, difficulties, and doubts. So all of us say with Thomas, the apostle, "My Lord and my God," and with the man seeking a cure from Jesus earlier in the Gospel story, "Lord I believe. Help now my unbelief!"

THE LOVE FEAST

by Andrew Greeley

WE know that Jesus ate and drank with his followers many times during the course of his public life. It seems likely that many of the parables and sayings we have in the gospel stories are "table talk," recollections of conversations when Jesus and his followers were breaking bread. It was thus perfectly natural that the two disciples at Emmaus would recognize Jesus in the breaking of the bread, for that act would recall their most familiar and intimate experiences with him. If someone we know very well had been gone for a long time (like the hostages in Iran, for example) and that person returned, seeming like a stranger, we might finally be sure he was the one we loved when he sat down to eat dinner with us. At dinner with our loved ones, we relax, put aside our masks and disguises and become ourselves. Sometimes that self is nasty and difficult; at other times, lovable and charming. Under such circumstances those who love us recognize us as the one we really are. This is surely what happened on the road to Emmaus.

The mass, or the Eucharist, grew out of the evening meals that Jesus had with his followers. They came together after Jesus had gone back to the heavenly Father to eat bread and drink wine and to remember the wonderful times when Jesus ate with them. It was after this custom had developed that they realized the significance of the final meal they had with Jesus on Holy Thursday and linked that with the "memory" dinners they were having. In other words, for a time in the early church the distinction between an ordinary evening dinner and the Eucharist was blurry. Even later on, when Paul was complaining to the Corinthians about their behavior at mass, the Eucharist was linked to and followed a banquet at the end of the day. Nobody, of course, wants to return to such customs, but it is helpful to remind ourselves that we should not make too sharp a distinction in our minds between what goes on in church on Sundays and what goes on around the family dinner table in the evening, for they are both love feasts. At both, Jesus is present—in a different way in the Eucharist, surely—but present in our evening meals as he is wherever a group of people are gathered together that love him and love one another.

The mass often does not look like a love feast. It doesn't seem much like a dinner. Yes, of course, we eat bread and sometimes drink wine, and we believe that Jesus is really present in the bread and wine. But it is not a dinner like other dinners we know. And often, if truth be told, our family meals are anything but love feasts. Everyone comes to the table, bringing with them their own particular variety of difficulties encountered during the day, everyone demands sympathy and attention, everyone is tense and sensitive, and no one seems able or willing to be generous, loving, and unselfish. We all expect love at our family meals, but we often find it hard to give love at those times. That Jesus might be present at our intimate and special love meals, such as the quiet wedding anniversary dinner of a husband and wife, we would be willing to believe. That Jesus is present at our supper table in a similar way as he was with the disciples at Emmaus seems hard to believe.

So we have to remind ourselves of a link between the Eucharist and our family dinners. One strong but accurate way of putting it is that we eat the Eucharist at mass on Sunday precisely so that our family dinners can become as loving as the most intimate and affectionate of love meals. We gather around the eucharistic table with the Lord and our fellow parish members so that, filled with his faith and his love, we may go home and love one another the way Jesus loves us. We may not exactly dash home from mass with the enthusiasm the apostles showed when they left Emmaus and returned to Jerusalem, but there should be something of the same love and faith and joy in us each Saturday or Sunday when mass is over.

Why are we not loving enough when we eat with those whom we love? It is mostly because we are angry, frightened, and insecure. We feel hurt, and we don't love because we don't feel loved. The whole idea of the Eucharist on Sunday is that it is an experience in which we ought to feel loved by God, by Jesus, and by our fellow Catholics. Because of the love we feel at mass we can then go home and love those who are most intimate with us without any fear that they do not love us in return. That's what it's all about. It is hard—oh, so hard—to practice it. Jesus knew how important eating a meal with loved ones was. That is why he chose the Eucharist as a way in which he could be remembered by those he loved. Therefore he calls us to come together every Sunday to experience his love. Then, safe and secure in that love, we can go home and love one another.

A GENERATION OF LOVERS

by Andrew Costello

ONCE upon a time there was an old grandmother who was known for her kindness, her wisdom, and her understanding. Not only did her grandchildren come to her with their feelings and their failures, but she often received phone calls from friends when they were having troubles.

Most of the time she was quiet and listened. But there was one thing she was tough about. Whenever someone felt like he or she was a failure, she automatically would say, "If you fail at love, you've failed big. But if you fail a driver's test or an algebra exam, of if your boyfriend dropped you, of if you thought two plus two was five, those things are nothing compared to love. Now, if you've failed at love, you've failed big."

Next came the question: "Now, you haven't failed at love, have you?"

She had learned her lessons from the school of life. A daughter's marriage had fallen apart and one of her sons was an alcoholic and still had not entered AA. But she knew down deep to the bottom of her feet that even though she had made her share of mistakes, she had loved all her children. She knew that she hadn't failed at love.

Themes from the Bible

"If you fail at love, then you've failed big."

Everything else in her life, compared to that, was small. She knew well the wisdom of the saying of Seneca and Tennyson and the thousands of others who quoted it, "Better to have loved and lost than never to have loved at all."

In John's Gospel we have the commandment to love our neighbor. The Christian is chosen, called, commanded, and commissioned to love. This is our ministry. This is our apostolate. Mothers, fathers, brothers, sisters, single people, all people are called to love.

Nietzsche said, "The last Christian died on the cross." Chesterton said, "Christianity has not been tried and found wanting, it has been found difficult and not tried." Each Christian is called to try to love his/her neighbor and prove both Nietzsche and Chesterton wrong.

Love means not playing any favorites: When Peter discovered that God does not play favorites, his walls came tumbling down. The same thing can happen to us.

People hate to hear that they play favorites but let's be honest, we all have our favorites. Now obviously we like some people more than we like others. Liking is not the issue. Loving is. Playing favorites, and ignoring those we don't like, especially when it comes to family, is a practice that can scar people for life.

Consider the following letter to an advice columnist:

"Please print this letter. I need to say something to my mother. She might not guess this letter is meant for her, but if it helps some other mother realize how she hurts her children when she shows favoritism, I will have helped somebody.

44

LET THERE BE LOVE

"Dear Mom: Do you know how I feel when you and Sis and I have a conversation and you never look at me? All your comments are directed to Sis—as if I wasn't even in the room. When I express an opinion you interrupt and ask Sis what SHE thinks. When she says something amusing, you shriek with laughter. I don't think I've ever made you laugh in your whole life.

"I realize Sis was your first born and I suppose it's natural to love the first one best, but must you show it so clearly in everything you say and do? I know I'm not as pretty as Sis, nor as bright and witty, but I practically break my neck trying to please you and I want so much for you to love me. Please, Mom, listen to me, I'M TALKING TO YOU."

The first step then is to admit that we are like Peter. There are people in our lives right now that we are neglecting and avoiding, and there are people in our lives right now that we have made favorites. We might or might not be aware of this, but admitting it is a good place to begin our conversion.

Love means dying for the other: In John's Gospel, we hear Jesus tell us, "There is no greater love than this: to lay down one's life for one's friends." The old example for this saying was that of a mother dying in giving birth to her child, or a soldier jumping on a "live" grenade. The new example are to be taken from everyday life, especially in a marriage and a family.

Love means dying for the other. Marriages happen because people are dying for each other—dying to be in each other's presence night and day.

Marriages die when couples stop dying for each other

and start living or dying for themselves or for something or someone else.

Love means dying—giving one's body and one's blood to the other. Or as we know to the core: love means sacrifice, the sacrifice of oneself.

Anyone in a good marriage knows very clearly what the sacrifice of the mass is all about—the giving of one's body and one's blood to the other.

And if a marriage brings forth children, a good family will only result when mothers and fathers and family members, as they develop, give of themselves to each other: their time, their energy and their presence.

And if we love each other, two effects, two results, two conclusions will take place.

(1) **Joy:** The happiest people in the world are those who give; whether it's bringing forth a child or teaching children how to deal with a failure. "A woman about to give birth feels sorrow, but her sorrow turns to joy when she brings forth a child into our world."

The next time you are at a graduation, don't look at the graduates. Look at their mothers. Look at their fathers. Look at their teachers. Look at anyone who gave of themselves to get the child to that stage.

(2) **Fruit that will last:** And the second result of love is that love is infinite. It produces fruit that will last. After all, God is love! When we give of ourselves to another, he or she receives something of God—and each gift of love leaves its creative mark. Love produces love. The songs the mother sings to her child are recorded in the memory

of the child; so too the sleepless nights the mother cared for that child when he or she was sick.

The next generation of mothers, the next generation of fathers, will be a generation of lovers, if this generation is a generation of lovers. And if we fail at that, we have failed big.

The old grandmother I mentioned in the beginning of this reflection challenges each of us, "If you want to be a winner, win at love."

GOD HAS NO FAVORITES

by Sean Freeman

THERE are two things which almost everybody prides themselves on having—a great sense of humor and an open mind.

But, as just as many of us know about others, these are far from universal qualities. Too many people who boast of their well-rounded sense of humor fail the final exam for accreditation in that department—when they find themselves on the receiving end of the ludicrously embarrassing, their sense of humor seems to go on vacation. In the same way, many of those who declare their minds to be open on all subjects find that they snap shut when something comes along that collides with any of their pet theories or carefully nurtured prejudices.

The ability to laugh at oneself is essential to a true sense of humor just as the really open mind is at least able to entertain the possibility of merit in something new, strange, or at odds with personal perceptions and convictions. And religion is perhaps the single most difficult area of life in which to keep one's mind open.

In the Acts of the Apostles there is an account of a visit paid to a Roman centurion by the apostle Peter. Like the centurion who asked Jesus to come to his home to cure his

48

son, Cornelius was a Gentile who was nonetheless God-fearing and devout. He even gave generously to worthy Jewish causes in the port city of Caesarea where he and his cohort were stationed.

All this took place in the weeks and months following Pentecost while Peter was preaching and working wonders of healing in the full flush of the Holy Spirit. He had just raised a woman from the dead in Joppa—about a day's journey from Caesarea—and his reputation was spreading.

Reading the Acts of the Apostles straight through makes it possible to appreciate some of the fascinating nuances which following the narrative in bits and pieces precludes. So much was happening to Peter, for instance, that he was obviously overwhelmed by both excitement and awe. He was hearing voices, seeing visions that might make a man fear he was losing touch with reality. Yet here he was praying that a dead woman might return to life and immediately she sits up and does just that. He must have been able to sense the parallel that was beginning to reveal itself between his life and that of Jesus. He traveled, he preached the coming of the Kingdom and the Good News, he and his friends were persecuted, he attracted crowds, he worked miracles—and eventually, like Jesus, he would be crucified.

Peter had learned the lesson of his own frailty in his denials of Jesus. A man not so humbled might have been puffed up with pride in these powers of his. But Peter was obviously in holy awe of what was going on. He was learning, probing, trying to understand. His mind was forced to remain open to the new and strange happenings and ideas he encountered. He struggled to see the meaning of the events overtaking him and their relationship with the words and legacy of Jesus.

As he stands on a rooftop early one morning in Joppa, praying before he goes down to breakfast, he falls into a trance and sees a vision of a great tarpaulin coming down out of the sky. It is filled with all manner of creeping and crawling creatures. A voice tells him to kill and eat some of these creatures, most of which were ritually forbidden as food by the Torah. Peter protests that he has never eaten anything unclean or profane. But the voice of the Spirit tells him: "What God has made clean, you have no right to call profane." This happens three times and leaves Peter pondering the significance of this latest revelation.

Then appear messengers from Caesarea who invite him to visit the home of Cornelius. The voice of the Spirit tells him to accept, and the next day Peter and some of his followers make the journey. Cornelius, who has had a vision of his own, has assembled his family and friends—Gentiles all—to welcome Peter. The centurion invites Peter and his disciples into his house, but this is strictly forbidden to Jews. Now Peter thinks he understands his vision and boldly breaks the law by entering the house and recounting the great events and meaning of the life of Jesus to the company assembled there.

He tells them what his vision has forced him to accept— that God has no favorites, no one is profane to him, that he loves all who are righteous, no matter what nationality.

And then, to the wonder of Peter's Jewish followers, the Holy Spirit comes to the Gentiles who at once begin to speak in tongues and praise God. Peter now sees the complete point of his vision and baptizes Cornelius and company on the spot, ignoring the fact that they are not Jews, not members of the chosen race, not circumcised.

Peter recognized that this was truly a momentous event, what has come to be called "the Pentecost of the Gentiles."

"Could anyone refuse the water of baptism to these people," he exclaims, "now they have received the Holy Spirit just as much as we have?"

Peter was subjected to severe criticism by the Jewish disciples on his return to Joppa, but he stuck by his actions and made them open their eyes not just to the possibility but to the fact that God is absolutely impartial in his love, just as he is prodigal in giving it.

Acts does not mention it, but Peter might well have asked the other disciples to reconsider and ponder the meaning of the parables about the laborers in the vineyard and the prodigal son. God's love is his to dispense as he will and to whom he will and is not to be constrained by our narrow standards of what is just and fair.

Let all of us latter-day Gentiles and sinners give thanks that God's love is as Peter said it most surely is.

THE POWER OF LOVE

by James A. Connor

IN the last century, when the British held India captive as the East and the West for a moment kissed in battle like the Yin and the Yang, the light and the dark, a Christian priest and his friend, a doctor who traveled with the British Army, met a Buddhist monk sitting beside a road in the foothills of the Himalayas, in a place that seemed to call for conversations on metaphysics, and there the three discussed the nature of all things.

"Everything is matter," said the doctor. "Look around you. What do you find? Matter. You can't see, touch or taste anything but matter. How can you believe there's anything else?"

"You're wrong," said the Buddhist monk. "Everything you've mentioned is only an illusion. It may seem real, but that's because your body too is an illusion, just as you are. All things are one. The other things, the things you can speak of in words, are only false images."

"I think you're both wrong," said the priest. "All things are love. God is behind everything in the universe, every plant, every start. Each thing was built out of love and for love. That's why human beings were created. What other purpose does intelligence have, if it's not for recognizing and responding to love?"

LET THERE BE LOVE

At that moment, the three men came to the top of a hill. They could see a whole valley below them, the green plantations, the river, the oxen pulling plows. The workers in the fields whistled to one another as they carried their tools homeward along the road. The sun was setting, just then touching the horizon. The mountains behind them turned pink, the clouds crimson, the sky orange. The disk of the sun, bright yellow, wavered as it disappeared. The evening star winked into being.

The men stood in silence, their mouths open. They built a cabin in those hills, lived together and remained companions, perfect friends, each knowing instinctively the thoughts and desires of the others, though they never said another word as long as they lived.

Julian of Norwich, the fourteenth-century British anchoress, had a vision of the Passion, of the great sacrifice of Jesus. "All will be well," the Lord told her.

This is the core message of Christianity. That all will be well. It is the will, the intent of God, that all men and women be saved. We forget this simple fact all too often in the confusion of our lives. How many people have left the Church because of a false image of a heartless, accountant God who weighs up every deed in a scale and judges us with a calculator in his hand? This image is an idol, not the face of the Living God. It's a rampant heresy we fall into time and again, a by-product of Pelagianism, long ago condemned, that has somehow burrowed itself into our Christian unconscious.

The fact of our lives, the fact of the Good News, is that we are born into this world already under the power of love. Love surrounds us and penetrates us. Love is the air we breathe. It is the light we see by. Anyone who comes to this realization will be like a nearsighted person who puts on a first pair of glasses and shouts, "So *that's* what the world really looks like."

The result of this sudden realization of being loved is true freedom and true zeal. We all have a natural response to someone who loves us. We want to love back. This response is the beginning of true conversion. It means we can focus on something other than our own sinfulness. We can look at God and give true praise and thanksgiving, rather than spending our lives beating our breasts over our failures, real and imagined.

And of course, we're inadequate. Anyone who looks at the sea or up at the stars knows that instinctively. We really are tiny creatures after all. But to know that we are tiny, and *loved,* gives us a dignity that springs from humility, not from pride. We don't have to be gods. We can be what we are.

How blessed our simple, half-ape, half-angel race is. We don't deserve it. But even so, the blessing is ours. If we follow the natural promptings of our own hearts, once we realize that we are already loved, even in the midst of our sins, then our freedom will allow us to be the kind of Christians we want to be. Of course, we'll still be sinners. But even sin can be turned into a badge of glory by the Living God. Jesus came to call sinners, not back to a slavish attention to the Law, a Law which cannot be obeyed in its entirety, but to a change of heart. And no change of heart can occur without a reason for such a change.

Selfishness is quite logical, really, but only from within

the framework of loneliness. Outside that framework, within the perspective of love, the logic of the world shifts, readjusts itself, and a new intelligibility comes into play. The universe, formerly a network of heartless forces, becomes a unity of compassion. All things are held in being by love. The stars and planets move in their orbits because of love. Human life can become an interplay of love and response, response and love. Who abides in love, abides in God.

Perhaps the most common spiritual disease of America is addiction. As a people, we grab onto any pleasure we can find to assuage the pain of being alone in the world. Alcohol, drugs, sex, money, fine cars, nice houses, jewels, work, work, work. We've simply forgotten the fact that we are never alone. Those who live alone professionally—the monks, nuns, and hermits of this world—proclaim that fact every day of their lives.

Christianity is seen by many people in our country as something ancient, unprogressive, not looking toward the future, but concentrating on its own inner workings. At best, the Church is considered a kindly old dame, a bit doddering, and all too worried about the dust on her mantle. At worst, the Church is seen as an invading foreign power, much more interested in politics and control than in conversion of hearts. To some degree, these impressions are our own fault. We've forgotten the core of our own Gospel. Within that core is the power that will make the world and all its disparate elements pull together, to become a universe that *means something*. That power is love.

Here is the story we have to tell: God so loved the world

that he sent his only Son to live in it, to suffer for it, to die like every human being, and to bring that world into oneness with the Trinity. If we tell that story, the Easter story, over and over, a million times, we will possess a gift for that world that can change the hearts of Marxists and capitalists alike, that can reach into the lives of American consumers at play and change them into spiritual women and men.

THE SOUNDS OF LOVE

by Daniel E. Pilarczyk

IN the movie *The Heart is a Lonely Hunter*, there is a touching scene between Mick Kelly and Mr. Singer. Mick is a young girl who is deeply fascinated with music. Mr. Singer is a boarder who lives in the Kelly house. Mick wants to share with Mr. Singer the joy that she finds in music, but Mr. Singer is deaf. So one day Mick brings her record player up to Mr. Singer's room and puts on a Mozart record. As the music plays, she gestures with her hands and arms, trying to give Mr. Singer an idea of what the music is doing. She makes big sweeping gestures as the music grows in volume and complexity, and smaller gestures when the music grows softer. Mr. Singer sits there and nods and smiles as he watches Mick. Then the record is over, but Mr. Singer keeps on nodding and smiling as if it were still going on.

Mick realizes that she cannot really communicate to him all that she experiences in the music. She can only give him some vague idea of what it's all about. But she did it because she loved the music and because she loved Mr. Singer and wanted to share with him the most important thing in her life. Mr. Singer knew what she was trying to do, but he also knew that there was more there than he was equipped to grasp.

Themes from the Bible

What God reveals to us about himself can be summarized in a few words: there is one God, and in God there is one divine nature and three divine Persons: Father, Son, and Holy Spirit. The Son proceeds from the Father, and the Spirit from the Father and the Son.

Basically, God wants us to know that he is not some solitary, cold being existing quietly and isolated, all by himself, but rather in his very own life he knows and loves in a way something like we do. God shows us that in God there is Father, source and power; that in God there is Son, the Father's full knowledge of himself known so deeply and expressed so fully that the Son has a personhood of his own; that in God there is love, a love between Father and Son so intense that it expresses itself as a Holy Spirit, distinct from Father and Son, yet binding them together in love. We call God a Holy Trinity, a Holy "Threeness," three Persons yet one in being God.

What God communicates to us about himself is important, but *why* God communicates is perhaps even more important. Let's reflect a bit about what the communication means.

At the deepest level, people communicate—that is, they reveal themselves to one another—because they love one another. In a family, parents will talk to their children about their own parents, about their own childhood, about things that happened long ago. They do this because they want their children to know who they are. They want to share themselves with their children because they love them. Friends do the same thing. So do a man and woman who are in love with one another. They tell each other about themselves, about their families, about their likes and dislikes, about what happened since they were last together. They talk about a lot of things that might seem inconsequential to the outsider. But they tell about themselves because they are in love, and being in love means sharing yourself with somebody else.

But we often find that total sharing today is impossible. Sometimes we simply can't say everything we would like to say. And sometimes the person we are sharing with simply cannot grasp fully what we are trying to communicate. How can a grandparent tell a four-year-old what it was like to grow up during the Depression? How can one friend tell another what it feels like to lose a parent in death? How can one lover tell a partner *everything* about who he or she is? It's not that the one communicating doesn't know about himself or herself. It's not that the one listening doesn't want to understand. Rather, it's that there is always more about us than the other can really grasp. There is always a communication gap between what we want to say and what gets heard.

It's the same with God. Poor God! God wants to share himself with us. He wants to be part of our lives and he wants us to be part of his. And so he tells us about himself. But so much gets lost in the telling! It's not because he doesn't know what to say, but because our understanding or receptivity is so limited. Poor us! We are like the deaf Mr. Singer, trying to appreciate Mozart through gestures because we can't hear.

How can we understand what it means for him to be the Creator of the universe when we can't understand how a poet writes a poem? How can we understand what it means for the Father to give himself completely to the Son when we have such a hard time giving even a little bit of ourselves to somebody else? How can we understand what it means for the love of the Father and the Son to be so great that it is as almighty as themselves when even the most generous human love is tinged with selfishness?

But in spite of the communication gap, in spite of the fact that we humans understand so little of what God tells us, he tells us about himself anyway. He tells us about his innermost being. And he tells us for one single reason: because he loves us and loving means sharing yourself.

However we have to be careful not to make God smaller than he is. Sometimes, when things happen to us which we don't understand, we are inclined to think that God doesn't really know what he's doing. Why did God let me lose my job? Why didn't he give me a better personality? Why did he let my parents get a divorce? Why did he let me get cancer? We don't know the answers to questions like these. But we do know that God is wiser and smarter and far greater than we are. We do know that we don't fully understand our human existence and that the reason for our lack of understanding is not because God isn't doing things right, but because we are so limited. God's reality, God's knowledge, God's will are all infinitely greater than our own.

There is still something else, a second thing that God wants us to pay attention to. God wants us to be conscious of his love for us. He loves us more than he can tell us. He love us more than we understand. He loves us to a depth we can't fathom and in ways we can't appreciate. But he loves us. That's why he takes the trouble to tell us about himself. That's why he shares himself with us.

THE LAW MAKES US ONE

by Daniel E. Pilarczyk

IN our civil society there are all kinds of laws. There is criminal law and civil law. There are laws governing the flow of traffic, the payment of taxes, the settlement of disputes between private citizens. All these laws are directed toward maintaining the rights of citizens and keeping pace in society.

There are all kinds of laws in the church, too. There is the canon law, which governs rights and duties in the church. There is liturgical law, which governs the church's worship throughout the world. We also refer to the church's moral teaching as law, because it gives us direction about how to behave. Some of the church's law is directed, like civil law, toward good order and the keeping of peace within the community. We would soon have chaos if every bishop governed his diocese according to his own lights, or if every priest made up the Sunday liturgy as he went along. Every community needs laws and directives so that people know what to expect, so that they know where they stand. But law in the church has a deeper dimension than mere public order.

All the church's law and moral teaching is intended to be a specification, an explication, an unfolding of the basic covenant that God gave to the new Israel on that Pentecost when the driving wind shook the house where the apostles were and when tongues of fire came down upon them.

That new covenant is the covenant of love between God and humankind brought about by the death and resurrection of Jesus. Through Jesus' love for his heavenly Father, expressed in his human life, through his obedience to the Father's will which culminated in his death, Jesus brought God and humankind back into a right relationship again. He straightened things out for us, not in some kind of supervisual and formal way, but by making us over in his image so that we are like God just as Jesus is like us.

Consequently, just as Son and Father are united in love by the Holy Spirit, so also are we embraced by God's love in the Holy Spirit.

To be Christian means simply to work out the implications of our life of love in the Spirit. We do that as the community of the faithful. The basic law that governs this community is the law of love, the kind of love that exists between the divine Son and the Father, between Father and Son in the Spirit. This law of love is the new covenant, the new way of being a people. It was promulgated when the apostles were publicly filled with the Spirit and announced the good news about Jesus and humankind to representatives of the whole world.

In the Christian community all law is an expression of love, an expression of the love of the Spirit that is the foundation of God's new people.

There are two facets of law in the church. First, the observance of the law, whether moral law, canon law, or liturgical law, does not make us pleasing to God. It does not earn us a place in his love and life. We do not make ourselves good and obedient and thus force God to take notice of us. Just the opposite is true. God loves us already. He gives us his life in Christ and unites us to himself in the Holy Spirit. The living out of our life in obedience to God's commands is not the cause of our salvation but the result: it is our response to the love that we have already received from him.

Second, all laws of whatever kind in Christian life have to be observed in the context of God's love for us and our love for one another. The laws don't exist for their own sake, but for the sake of expressing our love for God in the context of his universal community. Without love, God, and community, law turns into legalism. We get into legalism when the law becomes an end it itself, when we observe the law without acknowledging what the law is for. And everybody agrees that legalism is not in harmony with real Christian life.

But avoiding leagalism doesn't mean that we are free to disregard laws that we don't understand, or that we don't have to observe laws when they become troublesome or don't reflect our views about the way things ought to be. Avoiding legalism means that we need to look on law in terms of God's love for all of humankind, in terms of the well-being of the whole catholic, universal community of faith. Law without love quickly becomes oppression. But love without law quickly becomes sentimental enthusiasm, or self-deception, or corporate chaos.

LOVE AND THE TRINITY

by Henry Fehrenbacher

IN a city bus an agnostic lawyer noticed that the driver raised his hat on passing a church. To show his superior intelligence he asked the driver why he did so. The driver replied that he did so in honor of the Blessed Sacrament.

"And I suppose," continued the lawyer, "you even believe in the Trinity. Can you explain the Trinity?"

The driver answered: "I believe in the mystery most assuredly, but I cannot explain it. But can you explain to me how you move your finger?"

"Because I will it," rejoined the lawyer.

"Why, then," demanded the driver, "can't you move your ears?"

The lawyer was confounded, and hastened to leave the bus, when the driver, turning to another passenger, said, "I declare; I feared he would beat my argument by moving his ears. A man who will believe only what he can see and understand is little better than a jackass."

Prospective converts in their first encounter with the priest instructing them have the distressing knack of asking immediately the most difficult questions. One day a shoe salesman brought his fiancee—a Jehovah's Witness at that—and, challenging his religion, she at once demanded that he explain the Blessed Trinity.

"Oh, not again!" thought the priest. "Why can't these people start on something a little easier?" Even St. Augustine had difficulties trying to explain the Trinity. Everyone has heard the story that he was walking along the seashore pondering the mystery of the Blessed Trinity and wondering how to describe it in words. Nearby he saw a little boy, who had dug a hole in the sand, and kept filling a big shell with seawater and pouring it into the hole. When Augustine asked the boy what he was trying to do, the boy answered him, "I am going to put all the sea into that hole."

Yes, thought Augustine, that is like me trying to put the mystery of the Trinity into a few human words. He did, however, go home and write a book on the Trinity. We can know something and not love it, he said, but is it possible to love someone that we do not know? We can know God by faith, even though we have not yet seen him face to face. Therefore we can love God. Unless we love him first by faith we will not be able to see him in heaven.

In the fourth century St. Hilary wrote twelve "books" on the Trinity, but even if we could read his involved and lofty Latin we could still not understand this deepest of mysteries. Today's readings do not use the term *Trinity*. Neither Christ nor Paul ever used the term; it is not found in the New Testament, to say nothing of the Old Testament. The three persons of the Trinity are, however, spoken of an endless number of times. Jesus tells us to baptize in the name of the Father, and of the Son, and of the Holy Spirit. When most of the Fathers and Doctors of the church wrote on the Trinity they usually were defending the Son or the Holy Spirit against heresies that were denying their divinity.

The feast of the Trinity was not extended to the whole church until 1334. Pope Alexander II, who died in 1073, didn't think that a special feast of the Trinity was necessary because the Holy Trinity was honored every Sunday. The feast is a dogmatic one, not an organic part of the liturgical cycle of worship. But if we dropped the feast some people might not know when to make their "Easter duty," their annual confession.

We can say that the Father sees himself, and this image of himself, this expression of himself, or Word, is the Son, and that the bond of love between the Father and the Son is the Holy Spirit. What today's feast amounts to, though, is a burst of praise for God. After treating of the work of the three Persons in the Advent-Christmas-Epiphany-Lent-Easter-Pentecost season, we step back, look it over, and praise God for what he has done for us.

It is doubtful that anyone meditates on the "threeness" of God—except perhaps as a community of love. A bearded old rabbi once said, "God's dream is not to be alone." The Blessed Trinity is a community of love. Man, made to the image and likeness of God, is also created to live in a community of love. Christ speaks lovingly of his Father, and at the Last Supper he shows us his yearning to be with the Father.

Christ invites us to be part of that divine community

LET THERE BE LOVE

of love: "If anyone loves me he will keep my word, and my Father will love him, and we shall come to him and make our home with him" (John 14:23). Christ asks the disciples to make disciples of all nations, that is, to invite all people into this community. It is no longer just for the Jews; no one who wishes to join is excluded.

Baptism is the ritual that welcomes them into this community of love. Newcomers to the community are baptized in the name of the Father and of the Son and of the Holy Spirit. The Hebrew expression "in the name of" means into the very existence of.

Each parish, each monastery, convent or other religious house, each family strives to become a community of love. It is the work of all of us to strengthen community ties, not to break down those ties, not to separate people, not to alienate others. To cause divisions, enmities, strife, is a violation of our vocation as Christians.

"The Spirit brings love, joy, peace, patience, kindness, goodness, trustfulness, gentleness and self-control (Galatians 5:22). These are the qualities or virtues we need for building community. Again and again in every area in small and big ways we must work to build up community. It should become almost instinctive for a Christian. It must be painful to ourselves when we contribute in any way to disunity.

Paul told us that if we go snapping at each other and tearing each other to pieces we will destroy community. Such people, said Paul, cannot inherit the kingdom of God. They would not be fit for the eternal kingdom of love; they have no resemblance to the Holy Trinity.

Themes from the Bible

The scattered flock has been gathered together in the name of Christ. The people of the tower of Babel can speak again with the same tongue, the language of Christ and the Father, the language of love, the language of the Holy Spirit.

Only if we understand love do we have some understanding of the Trinity. Yet the more we think of love and experience love, the more of a mystery it seems.

Can we love what we cannot understand? asked St. Augustine. But can we understand love itself? Perhaps not, but we will not give it up on that account. There are mysteries in this life and certainly in the life to come. Let us resolve today to celebrate these mysteries as one of the all-too-often neglected wonders of our life, and let us celebrate especially the greatest mystery of them all, the existence, the goodness, the all-encompassing love of God as manifested in our concept of God as Father/Mother, Son, and Holy Spirit—a community without seams, an entity of perfection, a great sun of love into which we are all absorbed through our relation with Jesus Christ.

GIVE TILL IT HURTS

by Sean Freeman

"The joy of giving"

THE phrase has become so closely associated with fund raising and charitable drives that it has nearly lost its positive meaning for many of us. On hearing or reading the words our initial reaction is likely to be, "Oh no! How much are they trying to hit me for now?" And the reaction is completely understandable. Besieged on all sides by requests for donations large and small to humanitarian causes, civic action groups, "marches" for or against this or that—and, yes, also by the church, even the most willing giver has to draw the line. The federal, state, and local governments don't ask—they take in the form of ever-mounting taxes. For the sake of their jobs others feel impelled to give to certain agencies and funds because it is expected of them. Where, we can rightly ask ourselves, is the much vaunted joy in such giving?

One of the most consistent messages of the Gospels is that Christians, besides turning the other cheek and loving their enemies, are expected to be generous givers—givers of both their material and their spiritual bounty. The corporal and spiritual works of mercy are really nothing more than a detailed listing of the ways and areas where this Christian giving-til-it-hurts should be exercised.

Even in our largely depersonalized society where institutional giving has become the norm, it is still expected that Christians help their individual neighbors, brothers and sisters in times not only of need, but of loss, illness, death, and imprisonment. But, however regrettable, it is also the norm that when we think of giving we tend to do so in a purely material sense and usually in terms of dollars.

In the Second Letter of Paul to the Corinthians we hear one of the earliest recorded fund appeals. Paul had put much effort and time into establishing a sort of perpetual relief fund through which more affluent members of the early Christian community provided aid to the less fortunate. The Corinthians were evidently counted among the former and, because of both human nature and certain controversies in the local church, had lost a good deal of their original zeal for Paul's project. In today's phraseology, they weren't honoring their pledges.

But Paul does not rebuke them for this or shame them back into line. Instead he reminds them that they are among the most fortunate of people—they are possessed of a wealth of blessings which they should not count lightly. They have been given the faith, the eloquence to express it and share it with others, enthusiasm, and, not least of all, the largest share of Paul's own time and affection. He goes on by asking them to remember the generosity of

LET THERE BE LOVE

Christ who was, before he became man, possessed of the riches of heaven, but he gave them up and took on the far humbler nature of humanity and a life of poverty and suffering, so that he could, through his obedience unto death, bring them the riches of the heaven they can now enjoy.

He does not ask that they destroy their own lives for the sake of others but simply give from their surplus of both spiritual and fiscal plenty so that others may not be made miserable by want—by want of hope, charity, and the hearing of the faith, as well as by the want of hunger and need which, as surely as sin, can pull people down to the animal preoccupation with need to survive.

In the curing of the woman afflicted with a hemorrhage and the resuscitation of the daughter of Jairus, Mark shows us Jesus giving freely of his miraculous powers. In the case of Jairus, Jesus gave more than was asked or expected. The plea had been for a cure. When word comes that Jairus' daughter had in fact died, everyone, including Jairus, accepted the fact that it was now too late. But Jesus is not just given power over illness, but over death itself. Life is the ultimate gift, one which no one dreamed of asking for. Jesus gave it freely.

The case of the woman is posed differently. She did not ask Jesus to cure her but told herself that if she could but manage, in the terrible press of the crowd, to touch his robe, she would surely be cured—and she was. At first take, Jesus' reaction seems somewhat strange. It is almost as if he was angry that someone had "stolen" a cure from him. Or was it that Jesus, like many of us, preferred to give personally rather than anonymously?

71

Themes from the Bible

The answer most likely is that neither was the case. Jesus did not want to be taken for a mere magician. He cured through God's power and in response to faith in that power. By searching out and confronting the woman he made it clear—through her own account of her motives—that it was indeed faith that had released his healing power—indeed, faith of such an order that it did not even have to be formally articulated in order for him to respond to it.

Such is the magnitude of the Lord's giving of himself.

Perhaps it would bring back the joy of giving if we were all allowed to be free of pressures and constraints and thus able to pick and choose the objects of our generosity. But we should not let such pressures and seemingly endless demands for contributions of money blind us to the far more precious gifts we have to give as Christian people. When we offer help without being asked, when we give the best of ourselves freely—to our friends, our children, our wives and husbands, our co-workers—we are imitating the Jesus who cured the woman whose need was not even spoken. When, from the bounty of our present well-being, happiness and faith, we come to the aid of others who are ill, impoverished, handicapped, old, isolated, desperate, embittered, depressed, or bereaved, we are giving back some of the riches which Christ, through his great sacrifice, gave to us. There should not be smugness or self-righteousness in our giving, but there is absolutely nothing wrong in partaking of the true Christian joy of sharing our love.

THE STING OF REJECTION

by Sean Freeman

THERE are many worse things that can happen to us than personal rejection. But, while it is happening, there certainly doesn't seem to be anything in the world more painful. The child who's not selected for the cast of the nativity play, the young boy who's not chosen to be on either side of a pick-up game of touch football, the aspiring college student who is not awarded the scholarship, the girl who's not asked to the prom, the man who doesn't get the promotion, the love-sick suitor whose proposal is scorned, the author whose labor of months is returned with a curt note of dismissal by a publisher—all these people (and, in one way or another, at some time, we will all count ourselves among their number) know the burning shame, the just plain torment of rejection.

The psalmist complains of rejection from the haughty: "We have had more than our share of scorn, more than our share of jeers from the complacent, of scorn from the proud." This rejection is evidently inflicted on those who follow God's laws by those who totally disregard them.

Paul writes to the Corinthians in a context of rejection, too. A number of "false apostles" had set themselves up in Cornith during his absence and people had turned to

73

them and their more "flashy" teaching. Paul feels spurned but tells them he can endure it all because he knows the true nature of the revelations and special gifts he has been given by God. In fact God has given him a special afflic-tion—"a thorn in the flesh"—to keep him properly aware of his humanity and humility. "That," says Paul, "is why I am quite content with my weaknesses, and with insults, hardships, persecutions, and the agonies I go through for Christ's sake." And that includes accepting the rejection by the very ones he has ministered to at such heavy cost.

In Mark's Gospel, Jesus himself feels the sting of rejec-tion. He returns to Nazareth and, on the Sabbath, goes to the synagogue to teach. Today we are accustomed to taking literally the Gospel descriptions of Jesus' impact on those who encountered him. So, at first take, it is easy to assume that when Mark tells us the local people "were astonished when they heard him," he means that they looked on him with awe and wonder. This indeed may have been the case but a closer reading of the verses would seem to indicate something quite the opposite.

Instead of reading, "Where did the man get all this? What is this wisdom that has been granted him, and these miracles that are worked through him?" let's substitute a more contemporary version: "Who does this guy think he is, him with his high-and-mighty teaching and so-called reputation for working miracles? He can't fool us—he's just the carpenter's son. His relatives are all right here. What makes him think that he's better than any of them, or any of us, for that matter? He may get away with all this posturing and preaching somewhere else, but we know him for what he is. Who does he think he is to stand up in the synagogue and teach us?"

No? Then why does Mark add at once, "And they would not accept him"? And evidently Jesus felt that the full impact of the rejection because he tells them, "a prophet is only despised in his own country, among his own relations and in his own house."

This is an old and very human reaction and has been the theme of many a story and movie. The person who has become a celebrity or even a star comes home to find himself or herself not only just one of the people but actively scorned and resented "for putting on airs" even when such is not the case. This kind of rejection can be doubly painful, because one's hopes of a triumphant return and a little of the respect which was so longed for in the past is not only withheld, but positive resentment is thrown in one's face.

Mark says that Jesus "could work no miracle there in Nazareth." In Matthew's version, which sounds much more likely, "could work" becomes "would work." In the circumstances it must have been very tempting to the human side of Jesus' nature to put on a truly dazzling display of his divine powers, to work some really spectacular miracles that would show these yokels who he really was. But, of course, he resisted this temptation—if indeed it ever entered his mind. Instead he was simply amazed at the lack of faith he encountered—the hostility and resentment. Without the presence of faith he would work no miracles, put on no sideshow for the sake of unbelievers.

This would have been beneath his dignity and, more importantly, against the will of his Father. Besides, he was soon going to be on intimate terms with rejection of a far more serious sort. The sort of rejection that would bring about his death.

There really is no antidote for the hurt of personal rejection—after all, it is not just our work or ideas that are being spurned, but our very selves. One may get used to personal rejection—this has been the theme of many a "Peanuts" cartoon strip—but one never grows to feel indifferent about it. If there is a Christian approach to rejection, it would be to accept it as a lesson in humility and growth. If we can't manage that, then at least the Christian should resist the temptation to lash back with anger born of hatred for those who reject us. In this we have a clear example from Jesus when he resisted both anger and making a show of his divine powers on being rejected by the people of Nazareth. He was simply amazed by the lack of faith these people displayed. So it just may be all right to make a similar judgment about those who subject us to the pain of rejection. Perhaps they just don't recognize a good thing when they see it.

THE MEANING OF PEACE AND LOVE

by Henry Fehrenbacher

ONE evening a man walked into a dark room. As he opened the door and before he could turn on the light he saw the words PEACE and LOVE glowing in the darkness. He stood stock still in amazement. Was this a ghostly message from another world? Was this a heaven-sent prophecy, in this gloomy world, of good things to come? Or was it perhaps a fateful admonition? He recalled the Old Testament story told by the prophet Daniel of the handwriting on the wall. King Belshazzar, so the story goes, was giving a banquet for a thousand of his noblemen when a hand appeared in the air and wrote on the wall of the banquet hall the words MENE, TEKEL, PERES (Daniel 5:26).

But those words, the man reassured himself, were a warning to Belshazzar that he had been found wanting and that his kingship was about to end. Right on schedule, to fulfill Daniel's interpretation of the three words, the king was murdered that night.

Those three words, the man reassured himself, were a prediction of forthcoming evil. Peace and love are good things. Calmed by his self-assurance he turned on the light.

The man was a father who had walked into his son's

bedroom. And his mood quickly changed as he realized that the words he had seen were made luminescent by blacklight, and that they were crudely painted on a pull-over sportshirt that he had given his teenage son for his sixteenth birthday. "Ruined that new sportshirt," he fumed. "I'll add a third word to PEACE and LOVE and that word is BALONEY!"

Peace and love—great, beautiful, and immortal words—two of the few words of eternity, words describing heaven, words whose reality will never end because God, their author, will never end. Zechariah had prophecied that when our king and savior would come "the warrior's bow shall be banished, and he shall proclaim peace to the nations."

The Holy Spirit, the spirit of Christ, is the spirit of love, and from that love flows our peace. Peace is one of the fruits of the Holy Spirit, or rather, with love is the fruit of the Spirit. Paul uses the singular.

PEACE and LOVE no longer glowed in the dark, but the father could not erase them from his mind. His mood was dark, and the words seemed impressed upon his interior vision. "What do these words mean anyway?" he asked himself indignantly. "Ruining that new shirt."

But what do the words mean to his son? he had to ask. "Nothing," he said. "They are just slogan words of outdated hippies." But with the maturity of a father he calmed down. Perhaps, he reflected, his son wanted more than a thing bought from a department store. Perhaps he wanted more than a thing. Perhaps the son had added to

LET THERE BE LOVE

that thing, the sportshirt, the words indicating what he really wanted—peace and love.

It was easy to buy him the sportshirt, the father realized. It is much more difficult to bring him peace and love. According to Zachariah, peace, whether between two people or between nations, is a mark of the messianic kingdom. Though we yearn for peace it is not something passive. It is not the mere absence of violence and dissension. Great energy and effort are spent for war and proportionally little for peace. Yet Christ prayed for and died for our peace.

"I will arise and go now, and go to Innisfree..." wrote the great Irish poet, William Butler Yeats, in *The Lake Isle of Innisfree*. "And I shall have some peace there, for peace comes dropping slow, dropping from the veils of the morning to where the cricket sings." *The Lake Isle of Innisfree* is one of Yeats' earlier poems, and when he matured as a poet he was embarrassed by the popularity of this poem, for he considered it too romantic.

The poem was popular, though, and still is, because in writing of finding peace Yeats wrote of what interests most human beings. While standing on the crowded streets of London, "the pavements grey," Yeats felt that he could hear the sounds of peace—"for always night and day I hear lake water lapping with low sounds by the shore—hear it in the deep heart's core."

Our hearts yearn for peace, perhaps especially these days when the violence and dissension throughout the world are brought almost instantaneously by the news media into our homes and hearts. The insanity of deliberate yet mindless violence, the blowing up of children, the bombings in busy streets, the kidnappings and other terrorist tactics, so widespread today, make peace seem an impossible dream.

Even on a national scale we are able to unite a nation for war, but we seem to be unable to unite it for peace. We are adept at waging war, we continually make plans for war, we have military schools and camps for war, we pay scientists to devise more efficient means of killing people, we tax citizens outrageously for war, and with blast of bugle and wave of flag we sacrifice our young to war.

Nations do not think of making all that effort for peace. In contrast to the war makers, in contrast to those who destroy peace, who work for dissension and disunity, we have Christ who sacrificed himself for peace, sacrificed himself to reconcile people with God, and persons with persons. "Peace is my farewell to you, my peace is my gift to you," Christ told the apostles at the Last Supper.

Only if we are peacemakers will we have peace in our hearts. Blessed are the peacemakers, said Christ in the Sermon on the Mount. Even amidst the turmoil of the world we can have peace in our hearts if, filled with the Spirit, we are missionaries of Christ's peace and work for the reconciliation of humankind.

At the end of each day as we examine our conscience we must ask ourselves what we did that day to bring about peace and reconciliation. We may, if we are honest with ourselves, discover that in subtle, vicious, small ways we caused division, disunity, and enmity. We took revenge when we were cheated, lied about, made objects of gossip, deprived of what we justly deserved. At such times it is difficult to love, to forgive, to make peace. Yet we will not be happy, we will not be blessed, unless we do.

Peace is constructed in many small ways, and only when we have the peace of Christ in our hearts can we bring peace to others—for we cannot give what we have not got. When Paul describes the fruit of the Holy Spirit he puts between the words love and peace the word joy. That is the third word which the father in our true story should add to his son's sportshirt.

"I need some peace and quiet," we tell ourselves. The stated goal of many a vacation is to realize an interlude of this same peace and quiet. The implication is that real interior peace is as difficult to achieve in the course of everyday life as it seems to be to achieve public peace between nations in the world at large. We do not consciously say, "I need some peace and love and joy." Perhaps that is why we cannot find peace in our ordinary routines because they are devoid of love—the love we should be at pains to express to those we live and work with, the love which we look for in return. If we try to make contact with that love, make room for it in our lives, realizing, reflecting on the promise and hope that God has given us, then peace can come, love can come, joy can come—even in the midst of outer chaos.

WHAT YOU LOVE IS WHO YOU ARE

by William Herr

IT is difficult to open up a popular magazine these days without coming across one of those quizzes which are supposed to help us find out what kind of people we really are. There are quizzes to determine whether we worry too much, whether we have a positive or negative mental attitude, whether we have hidden feelings of insecurity, and on and on and on.

More than fifteen hundred years ago, Augustine developed a different kind of self-knowledge quiz. His quiz was very simple—extremely simple, in fact, because it contained only one question. Tell me what you love, he said—tell me where you seek your happiness—and I will tell you what kind of person you are and what kind of life you lead.

Augustine was aware that it is not what we believe which determines how we live; it is what we choose. It is what we love which reveals most clearly who we are.

This really is just another way of saying that our lives are made up of actions, and actions depend upon choices, and every choice presupposes a value. We are what we choose, and we choose those things which we believe to be more important than other things. If you know a person's values, you know the person. And if you really know your own values, then you know yourself.

LET THERE BE LOVE

We may never have stopped to consider what our values are, but we can be certain that we do have them. Someone who has no values at all could not even decide to get out of bed in the morning—and also could not decide to stay there. A person without values, in other words, simply could not live.

But it is not enough just to have values. What we also need, to use a word which has fallen very much out of fashion these days, is wisdom. We need the ability to make good decisions in cases where one value conflicts with another one. This is what Solomon was referring to when he asked for "a heart to discern good and evil," for evil is nothing more or less than the choosing of a lower value over a higher one.

If we lack the ability to make good decisions concerning values, there can be no pattern or consistency in our lives. What we do in the short run will not be in harmony with what we want in the long run. What we decide tomorrow will have no relation to what we decided today. We will just stumble along aimlessly from minute to minute and from day to day and from year to year. And, in the end, our lives will have been nothing more than a long series of unrelated incidents.

Wisdom allows us to prioritize our values, to establish a kind of hierarchy, so that those things which we believe to be less important will not interfere with those which we believe to be more important. At the top of this hierarchy must be one thing which we consider to be most important of all.

There are many varieties of wisdom. There is a kind of professional wisdom, which helps doctors, lawyers, and businesspeople to exercise good judgment in their occupations. There is a wisdom based on personal experience, which helps parents to become skillful and compassionate teachers of their children. There is a philosophic kind of wisdom, through which a person is able to lead his or her life according to a well-reasoned set of beliefs.

What we are primarily concerned with here, however, is a specifically Christian kind of wisdom—a way of life based on a Christian hierarchy of values.

It was values, after all, which Jesus spent his life trying to teach us. Jesus did not expound dogma, and he did not discuss theological propositions. What he did do was ask his followers to live their lives in accordance with the same values he himself embraced. By proclaiming a new set of values, Jesus endowed the facts of everyday life with new significance.

This new significance, this specifically Christian set of values, means that the Christian and the non-Christian live in two different worlds. They walk side-by-side in the same physical world, but they live in different value-worlds. The same facts of nature—birth, death, joy, suffering, work, marriage, sexuality—have different meanings for them.

This concept of two value-worlds existing side-by-side in the same physical world found its most classic expression in Augustine's masterpiece, *The City of God*. Augustine believed that the driving force of all human history has been the struggle between two communities, one founded on love of God and the other founded on love of self. Since their value systems are incompatible, these communities will always stand in opposition to one another.

LET THERE BE LOVE

It is not difficult to find examples of this conflict between Christian and non-Christian values today. We can see it in the best-selling books which proclaim that the way to become successful is not to love one's neighbors but to intimidate them, to Look Out for Number One. We are confronted with this conflict of values whenever we hear television personalities assert, either by word or by example, that qualities such as honesty, compassion, simplicity, kindness, and faithfulness are not the hallmarks of a mature and responsible person but the distinguishing characteristics of a weakling or a simpleton.

But the same kind of conflict between Christian and non-Christian values also can exist within a single individual, if he or she tries to live by two different standards at the same time. A person may be wise as an accountant or architect, or as a parent, or even as a philosopher, and yet be foolish as a Christian—a situation which Jesus described as trying to serve two masters.

We already have said that any coherent system of values must be founded on one supreme value, something to which everything else must be subordinated—money, perhaps, or pleasure, or power, or fame. A Christian value system is one in which nothing has any intrinsic importance except insofar as it leads one to God, through Christ.

As we grow to maturity, we learn to accept the fact that, in order to get one thing, you have to give up something else. If you want to become a great athlete, or a great artist, or a great scientist, you have to give up something. If you want to become rich, or have a successful career, or raise a family, you have to give up something. And if you want to be a Christian, you also have to give up something—you have to give up the values which the culture around you has adopted.

All of us have heard it said that everyone has his or her price, something for which every person would be willing to sacrifice whatever he or she holds most dear. Perhaps there are some people for whom this is not true, but certainly every Christian does have his or her price. And the Christian knows exactly what that price is. The Christian knows for what pearl he or she would give up all else.

This provides us with a kind of standard against which we can measure ourselves. Homilists might suggest the following to their congregations: Sometime this afternoon, or before you go to sleep tonight, set aside some time to take Augustine's quiz. Ask yourself what the most important thing in your life is. What are you willing to give up everything else for? What kinds of decisions do you make in the course of a day, and what do those decisions reveal about your own personal values? Are you living in the Christian value-world, or in another one?

It is possible that you will be satisfied with what you discover about yourself. But if you are not satisfied, remember that values are not like factual knowledge—they cannot simply be handed down from one person to another as can multiplication tables or the alphabet. No one can learn them once and for all. They must be acquired and retained through repetition, just like proficiency on a musical instrument.

Jesus taught us values, just as our parents taught us values and as those of you who are parents have taught your own children values. But this knowledge by itself will not make anyone virtuous, any more than hearing Arthur Rubinstein explain how to play the piano would make a person musical. Jesus pointed out a new level of reality in things, but it is up to us to open our eyes to that reality and to make it our own.

If we should discover that we have fallen away from the values which we want to live by, the reason probably is that we have lost sight of the relation between our everyday actions and the one supreme value to which those actions should be related. And we probably have lost sight of that relation because we have gotten out of the habit of rededicating ourselves to that supreme value each day. Acquiring that habit of rededicating ourselves—day after day after day—is the key to reorienting our lives around the values Jesus taught.

There is an old story about a man who arrives in New York City and asks a passer-by how to get to Carnegie Hall. And the passer-by tells him, "Practice, man, practice."

If you find that you have been accumulating many possessions, and letting the pearl of great price escape, there is no reason to despair or lose heart. Just practice. And practice.

THE LAW OF LOVE

by Daniel E. Pilarczyk

WHEN you buy a microwave oven, they give you a booklet of instructions. The instructions tell you how to turn on the oven, how to set the controls, what kinds of containers you should and should not use in the microwave. If you don't read and follow the instructions, you not only run the risk of not getting the most out of the microwave, but also of doing serious harm to it and perhaps serious harm to your kitchen as well.

When the doctor gives you a prescription, the pharmacist always puts on the package instructions about how much to take and how often. If we disregard the instructions, we probably won't get the benefit the medicine is supposed to provide and, in certain circumstances, we might even end up killing ourselves.

Our folk wisdom has the humorous saying, "If all else fails, read the instructions." That's true, of course. But it's much more intelligent to read the instructions *before* all else fails. Otherwise we run the risk of not having anything left to be instructed about.

One kind of instruction that has a significant role to play in our lives is *law*. There are several ways in which we can think of law, but the most fundamental is to look on

LET THERE BE LOVE

law as a collection of directions or instructions for living out our lives. If we follow the directions, if we are careful about the instructions, our lives will work pretty well. If we refuse to follow the instructions that law gives us, we can end up in a state of serious malfunction or even in a state of total destruction. Law isn't some sort of burden which society lays on our shoulders to keep us in line. Law isn't a set of rules which God has thought up to make us feel guilty. No, law is basically a set of instructions about how to love, how to behave in such a way as to function best both individually and in society.

For that reason, law is very important in the life of each of us. It is law that tells us we must not kill. It is law that protects our property. It is law that maintains order by telling us that we must drive on the right side of the street rather than the left. There are laws that tell us to go to church on Sunday, and there are laws which tell us how much of our income we have to turn over to the government in taxes. There are all kinds of laws, and all laws are intended to direct us to correct and productive lives.

At the same time, different kinds of laws call for different kinds of observance. Some laws, for example, call only for external observance. They determine behavior and nothing else. For example, the law says that we must stop when the traffic light is red. That's all we have to do. The law doesn't care whether we like it or not, it doesn't care if there is cross-traffic or not, it doesn't care if the only reason we stop is because a police car is right behind us. All the law calls for is compliance. These laws are called penal laws. We do what they say or we undergo punishment. They are not primarily concerned with what is inside us, but only with our external actions.

Other laws call for something more. The moral law calls for certain standards of behavior, but this behavior is supposed to arise out of certain dispositions of the heart. The moral law says that we must not kill. But it's not enough to refrain from murdering people. We are also supposed to love our neighbor in our hearts. We are supposed to respect our neighbor's life and person because of who and what our neighbor is, and because of who and what we ourselves are.

It seems pretty clear that if we confuse these two kinds of law there is going to be trouble. If we observe the moral law only in the context of external behavior, if we keep God's commandments merely out of fear of punishment, then we are treating the moral law like penal law. We are saying, by implication, that all God cares about is our outside performance, what we do or don't do. This kind of attitude not only overlooks the whole purpose of the moral law (namely, the growth and perfection of our heart and will), but it also makes God into some kind of heavenly policeman. It tends to turn our whole life into a game of cops and robbers in which we give great attention to how much we can get by with before we get caught, how we can use the technicalities for our own benefit, and what the minimum requirement is to satisfy the law. This is unfortunate because the moral law which God has given us is not intended to make us jump through hoops for him, but rather to foster and protect our life in him and our relationship with him and with one another.

LET THERE BE LOVE

Our attitude toward law, toward God's law in particular, is one of the basic elements which determine the quality and fabric of our life. There are four things we need to be clear about as we strive to carry out God's law.

The first is that we do not have to—indeed, we cannot—earn God's love in our lives by our good behavior. God loves us first. He gives us his life for our own in baptism. There is no way we can be worthy of him or buy his love. We receive everything from him as a gift. Our task is merely to live up to what God has given us.

The second is that the most important element of our life and action in responding to God's love is what lies inside us: our attitudes toward God and ourselves and our fellow human beings; our willingness to be open to the Lord; our desire to grow in his love. The goodness or evil of our hearts determines the goodness or evil of our lives.

The third thing we need to be clear about, always in the context of God's love for us and of the importance of the orientation of our heart, is that behavior is important. It is important as a manifestation and a confirmation of what is inside us. We can say we love God, but if we only turn to God in distracted and superficial ways, and irregularly at that, we are giving the lie to what we claim is inside us.

The fourth is that God's moral law is not the same kind of law as a traffic law. Its purposes are different and therefore the way we respond to it has to be something different than merely minimal observance.

It's important to read the instructions as we try to work out our lives. It's important not to wait until all else fails to attend to the instructions. But it is also important to know the purpose for which the instructions are given and to be willing to follow them out in accord with their intent.

NO MAGIC BUT LOVE

by Norbert J. Gaughan

MAGIC shows are always popular; they have suc-cessfully invaded TV. The magician known as David Copperfield gets a good-sized rating from viewers, and magicians who are good at their profession will win en-thusiasm and acclaim.

Basic to the magician's bag of tricks is the bit of "busi-ness" and the patter he does as he sets up and completes the trick. The magician's patter has a purpose. It is used to *divert* attention from the trick rather than to call atten-tion to it. But he gains our full attention in every little ges-ture by adding extraneous moves and extra words which add to the mystification. Some of these words have become enshrined in our language: "abracadabra" and "hocus-pocus." But these are always accomplished with gestures: the flourishes, the waving of colored scarfs, the quick move-ment of the hands.

When you hear Mark's Gospel story about the miracle of the "opening of deaf ears," as it is called, you should remember that this is one of the few miracle stories that seems to have Jesus doing extra gestures. Did you hear what the text told us? "He put his finger into the deaf man's ears, he spat, he touched the man's tongue." Jesus looks up to heaven. He utters a deep groan and says the words "be opened" in Aramaic.

This has led some people to speculate as to whether Jesus is not acting like a showman, whether he's not calling attention to himself rather than to the man in need of help. Yet, in Mark, who tells us this story, there is a reason for these actions of Jesus, and we'll come to that in a minute.

It is important to know where Mark located this story in his Gospel. Jesus has said just previously, "Listen to me all of you and understand." But the disciples closest to him do not understand that Jesus came to make men and women free from the regulations of the law. So Mark has, just before this story, given the example of the healing of a non-Jewish woman, the Phoenician woman's daughter. This was to demonstrate to the disciples primarily, and to all, that even the unbelievers now can enjoy the victory over sickness, sin and death that Jesus came to give.

Then comes this account which clearly, in Mark's view, fulfills the prediction of the prophet Isaiah: "Then will the eyes of the blind be opened, the ears of the deaf be cleared." That's precisely what Mark is demonstrating. It happens in Jesus.

The evangelist even does something most striking. He's the one who gives us these special directions about the route that Jesus followed from Tyre through Sidon to Lake Galilee, at which he arrived by going "through the territory of the Ten Towns." But as one commentator points out, that is a most unusual route to follow. It would be the same as if you set out from New York to go to Washington, D.C., by first going to Boston and then down the Mohawk Valley of New York State.

LET THERE BE LOVE

Was that the road Jesus took? No. Mark is telling us, by naming all the foreign lands around Galilee, what the miracle stories are saying: the message of Jesus, of forgiveness, of freedom, of healing from sin, is available even to the Gentile world—the very thing that Mark wants his readers, who are Gentile converts, to know.

Now we come to those strange gestures. Why did Jesus do that? We know he has said that God's work (and his) takes place in secret. God works quietly; God is not "show biz." But wait. Who is Christ healing? A deaf mute. This is the only way Jesus can communicate to the deaf mute. He is showing by signs what he wants to communicate. The deaf man cannot hear words, so what does Christ do? He uses these very gestures. Mark tells us all of this is done alone, away from the crowd, just between Jesus and the deaf man. Mark tells us that Jesus does "address the man." Notice, too, that the healing is done with a word, preceded by Christ's groaning. That groan echoes what Christ has previously demonstrated in Mark's Gospel. At human misery, the Messiah is moved to pity, he is pained at suffering. The man's deafness was not what God the Father wanted. The Aramaic word "Ephpheta" has come down in history and has even become part of our baptismal ceremony. Mark has put the Aramaic word there to symbolize the mysterious power of Jesus, and that by his Word the deaf man is set free.

For immediately the man is cured. The phrase "his tongue was set loose" still carries the notion that some evil power had bound up his tongue, and Jesus was unbinding that evil power so that the man could speak. We should remember also that Mark never actually uses the word

Themes from the Bible

"dumb." Rather, we are told the man had a speech impediment or, in another translation, "he could hardly speak." The cure is that he begins to talk without any trouble. This was the way God had wanted him to be.

Once more, we have Mark stressing the secret that Jesus is the Messiah. Then Christ tells the onlookers they are not to tell anyone. But that's a lost cause. With all his power, Jesus cannot stop them from speaking. But the time for *him* to speak plainly has not yet come. Mark will have Jesus make the announcement later. Yet God's revelation is recognized. It cannot be stopped among the people.

But when they speak, of course, nothing happens. It doesn't change anything. The people simply echo Isaiah, who hinted that the salvation time promised by God would come; now it has begun. It is only after the Passion, Death, and Resurrection that the ears, eyes, and mouths of men and women will really be open to God, when they see God revealing himself in the sufferings of Jesus.

So what lesson of faith does this Gospel story have to tell us? It stresses something we keep forgetting: that the way God deals with us in Jesus is always accommodated to each individual's needs and abilities. Notice in the case of this man, Jesus' actions just prior to pronouncing the word of healing were for the benefit of the man being healed. He had no other way to understand what was going on. But Jesus made it clear to him, so much so that when the command "be opened" was given, the man was ready to respond in faith and be cured.

There is an unfortunate tendency both among church people and among individuals to think that God acts the

LET THERE BE LOVE

same way with everyone. Or that we must all follow the same path to meet God. That's not what the Gospel story tells us. Jesus adapted the style of what he was going to do to the present situation and need. He was not doing this for the benefit of the crowd, but for the man in trouble. In so doing, Christ was able to win the response of faith from the man. This was a prelude to the healing.

Just read any part of the Gospels depicting the miracle stories. They are all varied. The Lord acts in different ways for diverse situations. For the Gentile woman who was worried about her daughter, Jesus got into a loving argument with her, and admittted her faith was great. When he cures the blind man, according to Mark, he does the healing by stages; that is, the man is not cured all at once, but has his vision restored gradually. In the other Gospels, in every case, Jesus goes one-on-one, modifies his style to the needs of the one in trouble. He takes time, he dialogues, he leads to an admission of faith.

That's something we should ponder, first of all, even in the raising of our own children. Yes, parents make house rules, general rules for everyone to follow. But they must be ready to bend them a little according to the different needs or problems of the child at any given time of life. In our human dealings with people who seem to have forgotten God or rejected him, we cannot just use a technique close to excommunication. We must work with each soul personally, and discover what actions are best to bring about desired results of change of heart.

Confessors understand that. They have heard confessions from such a variety of individuals. They know that no two human stories are alike, and they follow the healing style held up by Jesus which is adapted to the person and not to the confessor.

When we read this miracle story and remember Jesus' way of dealing with the man who could hardly speak, let's see it as a sign of the way God treats each one of us. In fact, he knows us better than we know ourselves. Sometimes we demand too much of ourselves, or we will not even grant forgiveness to ourselves. But he will because, you see, he knows us individually.

Let magicians use their patter, their many gestures. They are working out their magic. But in the healing of humans, there is no magic, no wonder show. There is no "abracadabra" with Jesus, no "hocus-pocus." Rather, he is the divine physician who knows our ills immediately. Believe that he is willing to excuse anything we do as long as we turn to him in faith and in love.

HE AIN'T HEAVY, HE'S MY ENEMY

by Daniel E. Pilarczyk

THE trademark of Father Flanagan's Boys Town in Nebraska is the image of a little boy being carried by a somewhat bigger boy, who is saying, "He ain't heavy, Father, he's my brother."

Whatever the historical background of the image may be, its implications are warm and comforting. We are invited to imagine that both boys were in some kind of deep trouble. They had no place to go, and they couldn't stay where they were. They had to find help. And they went for help to the kindly Father Flanagan, even though getting there meant that the bigger one had to carry his brother on his shoulders. It's a scenario that speaks of the kindness and generosity of the founder of Boys Town, as well as of the brotherly love and self-sacrifice of the boy who carried his brother on his shoulders to get to where they needed to go.

The bigger boy's dedication is unquestionable. Yet, if one thinks about the matter, he really didn't have much choice. At some point in their journey, the younger child simply couldn't go any further, but they had to move on. The options of the older boy were to leave his own brother behind to perish, or pick him up and carry him. He picked him up and walked with him, how far we don't know. Obviously it wasn't easy. But there was no choice. It was his brother. That's why he didn't seem heavy.

In the Gospels all of us are called to carry our brothers and sisters when the need arises, whether they be heavy or not, just because they are our brothers, just because they are our sisters. We owe love to our brothers and sisters no matter what the circumstances. There is nothing at any time that allows us to stop loving. The love we owe is a debt which can never be paid off in full and then forgotten.

Even when we suffer harm from those around us, we still owe them love. It's a special kind of love which is called forgiveness. Forgiveness means "loving in spite of." In spite of what another person has done to us, in spite of the pain we have suffered, in spite of the harm we have undergone, we are still called to love. That's what forgiveness means.

But forgiveness, "loving in spite of," does not mean that the harm our neighbor does to us is not real. Nor does it mean we must allow our neighbor to continue harming us. Doing harm to us is harmful to our neighbor as well as to us, and the debt of love that we owe calls us to help our neighbor to stop doing harm to him or herself. It's not a write-off process Jesus offers us, but rather a call to deal with our neighbor in such a way that our neighbor realizes what he or she is doing to us as well as what is happening to him or herself in the process. Jesus teaches us a way to love our neighbor "in spite of."

Sometimes, it is true, the best thing is to let the hurt go by, to turn the other cheek, to be patient, prayerful, trusting, to forgive without making a big issue of the matter.

LET THERE BE LOVE

But not always. Sometimes, for the good of the offender, we need to confront. We need to lay out our hurts and injuries and try to get the offender to realize what is going on. If that doesn't work, we have to try to get help, help from other persons, help from the community of believers. And if that's not enough, the offender can even be put outside of the community for a while until he or she realizes just how destructive his or her behavior is.

In this procedure the goal is not punishment. The goal is not to make the offender feel bad and make ourselves feel good. Rather, by our love and concern we seek to win the offender away from self-destructive and unjust behavior. The goal is reconciliation and the restoration of a loving relationship. We owe this to the offender because the offender is our neighbor. We owe the offender our love, no matter what the offense, no matter how often it is committed. We are called to forgive, to love in spite of, and there are times when open confrontation of the offense, for the sake of the offender, is the deepest level of loving.

There are two dangers we face in the context of confrontation. The first is to refuse to confront a situation when confrontation is obviously called for. "Yes, I know my husband or wife drinks too much. Yes, I am quite sure the neighbors are abusing their children. Yes, I am aware my boss treats me and everybody else like dirt. Yes, I agree that our local civic leaders don't do much for people who are without a decent place to live. But if I keep quiet, maybe it will all change. I'll just try to continue to be a nice, loving person and keep my mouth shut. That's all that God expects of me." That isn't so. Sometimes God expects a lot more of us in the context of loving our neighbor. Sometimes God expects us to stand up and *do* something out of love for our neighbor, the very neighbor who is doing harm to us, to others, to him- or herself. Often enough, the debt of love we owe to brothers and sisters simply cannot be paid by suffering in silence.

The other danger we face in confrontation is to confront because it makes us feel good. "I'm going to tell that so-and-so. I don't care what he thinks. I don't care what she does. I've had enough and I'm not going to take any more. I know I'll feel better when I've had my say, no matter what it does to him or to her or to them." Loveless confrontation may indeed give us a certain psychological satisfaction, but that is not what Jesus calls us to. The purpose of confronting another's wrong is not vengeance or getting even. The goal is to help our neighbor change bad behavior because we love that neighbor. Loveless confrontation is, at best, a harmful self-indulgence. At worst, it is abuse and hatred under the guise of virtue.

We are all called to carry our brothers and sisters. Sometimes they "ain't heavy," sometimes they are. But whether they be heavy or not, we owe them our love, we owe them our care, even when they hurt us, maybe especially when they hurt us. As followers of Jesus we have no choice.

THE PRICE WE PAY

by Timothy Fitzgerald

WHAT does it cost to get married? Anyone who has celebrated a wedding recently knows that it's not cheap. The cost of invitations, reception, flowers, and all, quickly adds up.

But consider the question in a deeper sense, beyond the trappings of a wedding: what does it cost to get married? What does it cost the individual to be married? At a retreat for married couples, that question was posed to the participants. Without a moment's hesitation, one fellow blurted out, "It costs plenty!" People laughed, teased him about his abrupt reply—but not one person disagreed with his assessment.

People pay a price for marriage. They sacrifice freedom, autonomy, privacy, free time, the ability to call their own shots. They learn that sacrifice and even suffering inevitably come their way because of that commitment. They discover that their priorities get challenged and changed. They find out that the cost of commitment is very real.

One of the challenges of marriage preparation is to help engaged couples recognize what marriage will teach them: to make a commitment like marriage carries a real price. The same can be said about other commitments as well:

103

Themes from the Bible

priesthood or religious life, friendship, parenthood, or career development. With any of these, one needs to consider the cost beforehand, to recognize that mature commitment exacts a steep price.

These are hard words, sobering words, and they are meant to be. If we proclaim and celebrate the joy of marriage, of religious life, of parenthood, we must also announce the price of such commitments. To forget or ignore that side of commitment is to ask for trouble.

As they journeyed toward Jerusalem, Luke tells us, Jesus tried to teach his followers about discipleship. Step by step, Jesus has shown them the implications of following him, the consequences of walking along this way. These are not easy words that he speaks to them now.

Consider the cost of this journey, he tells them, the cost of following me. It means sacrifice, transformation, being humbled. It means disavowing wealth and personal gain, preferential treatment. It means being called servant, rather than lord or master. Step by step Jesus shows us the cost of this commitment, and that cost is nearly more than we can accept.

If you want to be my followers, we have heard, you must deny yourselves, take up your cross daily, follow in my steps. Sacrifice, faithfulness, letting go, emptying oneself, following the Lord and not leading him: this journey to Jerusalem may be a lot longer and more demanding than we bargained for.

Discipleship costs plenty, and we must be aware of that. Luke's Gospel brings us back to those demands of Jesus, and reiterates them in even stronger terms. Disciples are

called not only to deny themselves, but to renounce possessions, and even to "turn their backs" on family. What are
we to make of it all? How serious is he?

We have to recognize what Christ calls us to by these
words: be people who are so consumed with following me
that everything else is secondary. Be followers whose preferential love for me entails leaving behind all else. Be disciples who surrender all claims to independence or
autonomy, who come to me with empty—and open—
hands. Be witnesses who daily share my way of life: emptying oneself as a servant, carrying the cross, following me
and not leading.

Jesus' words force us to look at our loyalties, our
priorities. Discipleship calls us beyond our own home,
family, backyard, parish, county. It's not that we are called
simply, or literally, to reject family. Rather, we are called
to make sure our concerns and horizons are not parochial
or provincial or nationalistic as followers of Christ. We
disciples are called to grow in love, toward the point where
all people are our brothers and sisters—no longer strangers
or foreigners or enemies. Christ calls us to reject an "Us
versus Them" or an "East versus West" or a "Haves versus Have-Nots" view of the world. He calls us to remember
that our priorities supersede family, nationality, race.
Christ challenges us to see life and human solidarity as more
important than national security or American interests.

Is it "family" Christ demands we reject? Or does he demand instead that we broaden and deepen and expand our
loyalties, our compassion, our concerns for the whole human family? How would Mother Teresa define the "fam-

ily" she feels loyalty toward? How would Archbishop Tutu describe the "family" he commits himself to? How would this parish define the "family" it witnesses to by word and by deed?

Christ's words address our atittudes about possessions as well, to realize that what we own can very easily end up owning us. We are in danger of divided loyalties, in danger of being enslaved by our possessions. In the midst of the Consumer Society, how do our Christian values fare? How do our loyalties hold up? Do the poor find in us generous friends? Are we better known for our generosity and compassion, or for our exotic vacations? What did any of us spend on lawn care in the past year? By comparison, what did we contribute to charity in the past year?

Possessions promise us security. But like any false good that promises security, this false god of possessions demands bigger and bigger sacrifices and offerings. We as individuals, as a parish, as a nation, can end up selling ourselves in order to sacrifice to this false god. It is the Lord who says to us, Beware! We cannot serve two masters, and possessions are a direct danger to discipleship.

These are hard words that the Lord speaks to us, as we walk with him toward Jerusalem. His words are unsettling because we know it's not simply "family" or "possessions" at stake here. At stake is whether we are serious about following him. Acknowledging that we are called to live by different standards and different loyalties is the issue for us. And we have to decide if we can do that or not, if the cost is worth it or not. Commitment costs plenty, the man at the retreat said. He sure knew what he was talking about.

Think for a moment of people in our midst, in our parish, who are examples of commitment and dedication like this. Think of the catechumen whose hunger for faith and desire to be part of the church cause alienation with a spouse or with parents who don't understand. Think of the family better known for its generosity to the poor than for its possessions. Think of the couple whose marriage has seen great suffering—alcoholism, a rebellious child, or a chronic disease—and where faithfulness, day by day dedication, has prevailed. These are people who understand the words of Jesus—denying self, leaving behind family, renouncing possessions. These are people who witness what Jesus is calling all of us to.

That single-mindedness, that commitment, is the call and standard and challenge for us all. The heart of the disciple sees the cost of such commitment, and knows that the cost is worth it. It is the heart of Paul, led by discipleship even to prison, to being a "prisoner for Christ." Yet Paul could still proclaim that he counted all as loss when compared to finding Jesus Christ. The heart of the disciple weighs things from new and different priorities. It is the heart enlightened by wisdom beyond conventional wisdom, by the "wisdom from on high".

The disciple is the one who knows the cost is worth it. The disciple is called to be "more than a slave," as Paul says to Philemon; called to be a "beloved brother," a beloved sister; called to "as a partner"; called to be one who follows and reflects the example of Jesus Christ. And the Christian disciple is one who freely chooses this, who considers the cost beforehand and says yes to this commitment. Love prompts a man and a woman to declare their free and conscious commitment to each other, no matter what the cost. Faith, in the same way, prompts us to declare our free commitment to follow the teacher, no matter what the cost.

Luke and Paul lead us to examine the challenge of discipleship. They also lead us to examine our response to that challenge. They give us the invitation, the measure, and challenge us to grow toward that. The question is not, "Is Jesus serious about these demands?" The real question is, "Are *we* serious about them?"

ALL IT TAKES IS LOVE

by Henry Fehrenbacher

ONE day there was a great rumpus in hell; in fact, there was so much noise that St. Peter heard it and he asked one of the angels what it was all about. So the angel went down to check up on it. When he returned he reported to St. Peter that one of the inmates claimed that it was a mistake that she was there and that she did not belong there.

She said that she had always been a rich and respectable woman and her sentence to hell was a mistake. "That's not likely," observed St. Peter. But still there was such a clamor in hell, with the woman screaming that it was a blunder to put her there, that she had always been respected and rich, so that finally St. Peter sent the angel back to ask the woman if she had ever done a kind deed in her lifetime.

When the angel confronted the woman with that question the woman merely started shouting that it was a mistake that she was there, and that they had better get her out of there immediately. But the angel persisted with the question: "Have you ever done anything kind in your lifetime?" So the woman shut up and she thought and she thought and she thought.

Themes from the Bible

Finally she said, "Yes. Once a tramp came to my door looking for something to eat and I gave him an onion." So the angel reported back. St. Peter said, "Well, an onion is something. So, go back, take that onion and hold it out to her. Tell her to hold on to it and in that way you will draw her up to heaven." So the angel did as he was told. He told the woman to hold on to the other end of the onion and he began to lift her up out of hell.

But the other people in hell saw her rising so they began holding on to her skirt, and others hung on to others, and soon the angel was lifting the whole population of hell out of the infernal kingdom toward heaven. But when the woman saw that, she was indignant and she screamed at them, "Let go! Let go, all of you! This is *my* onion!"

As soon as she said that the onion broke in two and she fell back into hell with all the others. Since then, St. Peter pays no attention to her, no matter how much noise she is making.

The moral of the story should be obvious. Heaven is the place for people who love and hell is the place for people who do not love. In fact, this is what makes hell *hell*—there is no love there. To live without love is torture. Even when the woman gave an onion to a hungry tramp she did not do it out of love; she did it maybe just to be rid of him. She still did not have love in her soul, so the onion, not given in love, could not be a means of taking her from the loveless place called hell.

Love covers a multitude of sins (1 Peter 4:8), and even the perfect act of contrition is really an act of love. But an old pastor one day complained that all we ever hear about in sermons today is love. "I am sick of loove, looove, loooove," he said. Perhaps he was thinking that we treat the subject of love too simplistically.

In fact, in one parish young people were in the parish hall making banners for the church, and the banners had the words "love, peace and community" emblazoned on them. But as they were making them there were disagreements about how to design and fashion the words and the disagreement ended up in a big fight and the banners never got finished. In one way the incident is rather humorous, but it does show that love is not merely a word for the lips, it must be in the heart.

We may get tired about hearing about love in sermons and homilies today, but the word is given hundreds of times in the Bible, perhaps more than any other word. Christ, we have heard so often, said that love of God and neighbor are the two great laws. And he was quoting the Old Testament when he said that. John says that God is love (1 John 4:9). And Paul says all the commandments are summed up in this, "You shall love your neighbor as yourself."

So it is difficult to read and meditate on the Bible without coming across the word *love*. We may think it to be overkill, but it was the Holy Spirit who inspired the Bible, we didn't.

Perhaps the idea is in the Bible so often, perhaps Jesus and the New Testament writers stress it so often, because it is so difficult to convince us that love is paramount. The Old and the New Testament are the accounts of God's love. Also, love is often difficult and we may find many things in the Bible and especially in Christ's message that we can

accept and we may get comfortable and then again that
word *love* comes along.

There is simply no way around it. If we do not love our
neighbor then Jesus will not accept our love, for true love
does not discriminate against anyone. And we cannot think
of anyone whom God does not love. The servant is not
greater than the master, says Jesus, so is there anyone
whom I do not love?

God does not expect us to have a wild, emotional love
for each person whom we come in contact with. That is
impossible. But each of us can think over the number of
people that we have come in contact with during the past
day and we can evaluate our love for each person. How
did we treat each person? Were we warm and friendly,
indifferent, cold, routine, sympathetic, snobbish, casual,
cheerful, mildly interested, concerned, bored, antagonis-
tic, pleasant, unseeing, resentful, cool, strictly professional, etc.?

Next, what would Jesus' reaction be to each person he
came in contact with? No, he could not gush over each
one. But there would be love in his eyes. These are people
he would suffer and die for. He could be indifferent to no
one. Even to dissuade the wicked man from his ways, as
the prophet Ezekiel urges, must come from love. And to
correct a brother who has done wrong, as Jesus urges, must
come from love.

One nice thing about God's commandment of love is that
we do not have to worry about whether any person is
worthy of our love or not. We don't have to make decisions or judgments. We don't have to analyze. We don't

have to worry about whether we are making a mistake. We don't have to take responsibility. All we have to do is love. Because God said so. We don't even have to memorize the ten commandments or "words." Paul says that love is the fulfillment of the law; the commandments are all summed up in the command to love. All I have to do is love. That takes a load off my mind.

Existentialist philosopher Jean Paul Sartre said, "Hell is other people." According to St. Paul, Sartre had it just backward: "Heaven is other people"—or our path to heaven lies in loving other people as we love ourselves. Nor does love consist in never having to say you're sorry. Saying one is sorry for rudeness, thoughtlessness, anger is very much a part of love. But the worst sin against love is simple indifference—treating people like they are simply not there—not there as human beings, that is. Affirming the worth of our neighbor by simple, warm acknowledgment is part of the commandment to love. And the Gospels make it clear that our neighbor is every person we meet, whether he or she be a supermarket clerk, the paper boy, or our own friends and relations. We needn't be a glad-hander or backslapper to accomplish this—a nod, a smile, a look of concern, a word in passing should be our resolve to bring this minimum bit of love into the world every day.

THE IDEAL OF LOVE

by Mary Peter McGinty

BILL and Susan are celebrating their fifteenth wedding anniversary. They have taken a long weekend to retreat to the solemn beauty of Door County and just to be together. The years have brought them well along the way to becoming "one body." Yet, both of them are struck by the way in which this is happening—a way so different from the ideal they pictured as they entered into marriage on that day long ago.

There have been many joys to share—the delight in discovering each other as unique persons; the amazement at the birth and growth of their two children: Chris, now entering his teens, and Jill, collecting ribbons as a champion swimmer; the excitement of new homes, new jobs, new friends; the sharing of deep faith and of genuine reaching out to help those in need.

Yet, what really served to weld them together was not the happy times—the tasteful moments that keep hope alive—but the disappointments, failures, frustrations, crises, tragedies that called forth every ounce of commitment and courage. As they look back over the years, it becomes clear that the union grows in the willingness to share, to survive, to confront the unexpected, the undesirable, the unchangeable disasters of ordinary living.

114

LET THERE BE LOVE

The temptation in such situations is to spare the other person from suffering, to tough it out, to go it alone—or to share it with someone else, thus jeopardizing the marriage relation. Bill and Susan have been through those trials, but fortunately have discovered their strength in bearing difficulties together, turmoils and disruptions yielding to trust, honesty, genuine concern and prayer. After fifteen years, a quiet peace is beginning to merge two persons into "one body."

The past year had been one of the most trying—enough to tear apart a family with weaker roots. Susan was diagnosed as having a life-threatening illness which began to consume everyone's attention, time, and energy. Not only Susan, but each member of the family in turn had been angry, resentful, unforgiving. The demands seemed at times to be unreasonable and unfair. One or another family member would react by staying away from home, by being too busy to help, by withdrawing from family togetherness. Bill and Susan carefully and gently talked their way through the crisis, and gradually let their acceptance seep into the lives of the children. When a transplant solution became available, the initial joy and enthusiasm quickly faded into the reality of trauma and life-long struggle. Bill and Susan shared all the aspects of their new situation with the children, becoming a stronger unit through the anguish.

With this ever-present tension, the year unfolded with the last illness and death of one grandparent, the trauma of major heart surgery for another. Bill was offered and accepted major responsibilities in his work; the family sold their home and moved into a new house; Chris came to a mature decision affecting his future by choosing and being accepted into a high school for next year. Disruptive? Destructive? Demoralizing? Yes, there were many difficult days; yet, the family is stronger; Bill and Susan can feel their oneness. The joys are treasured moments, the disruptive has come to be accepted. Most importantly, each person has become very special to the other—essential to their ability to live.

What underlies an experience such as this? A deep faith which gives meaning to relationships and specifically to the marriage covenant. A covenant such as marriage is rooted in the origins of the human race and in the God who creates in and for love. It is clear that the human person is created by a social being—one who needs others to be able to live humanly in the world. It is also evident that man and woman are meant to complement one another—their relationship is directed toward union. They are destined to grow into "one body"—as an expression of the love and the self-gift which are unique to the human person.

Within the culture of Old Testament times, it is somewhat astounding that the writers could so clearly express the identity of woman—she is not just another creature, but she is all that man is, fully human and meant to experience the intimacy of union. Genesis presents us with the ideal of marriage: nothing is to be more important than this union. One's spouse and family come before everything else. It is to be an intimate union: not a surrender of one to the other, but a sharing of life. The stability of the union is meant to be a major concern and top priority in all decisions. God wants his love to be present in human experience—this growth toward union is the most powerful human experience of that love. "That is why a man leaves his father and mother and clings to his wife, and the two of them become one body."

Paul, in his Epistle to the Hebrews, strengthens this ideal of the marriage relationship focusing on the Incarnation and on suffering. Marriage is compared with God's relation with us. He enters into a personal union with humanity, becomes fully what we are, gives himself totally to become one person, Jesus Christ. It is not a surrender, but a union of Word and flesh. A further comparison is seen in the relation of Jesus with the men and women who are Church: a union so intimate that they become one body. The marriage bond, the ideal of love, has very deep roots!

Yet, what also becomes evident in the experience of Jesus is the importance of suffering in the growth of a relationship. "Christ was made perfect through suffering." In a very real way, he was more fully united with us through the experience of difficulties, frustrations, and death. The ideal of human love is certainly attractive; it is also rigorously demanding.

The Gospel of Mark protects the ideal of the marriage union, even in contrast with Mosaic tradition. Moses allowed a man to divorce his wife; Jesus says that either husband or wife who divorces and remarries is guilty of adultery. The legal possibilities do not reflect the ideal of the marriage covenant. "What God has united, man must not divide."

What are we to learn from the experience of human living and the wisdom of tradition? That human friendship, with its paradigm in the marriage covenant, is an experience in self-giving. It can be destroyed by a focus on "my needs," on "my rights"; it can be enriched by a patient and gentle discussion when difficulties arise. It can be humiliating when one person exploits and manipulates the other; it can be uniquely fulfilling when each one is willing to listen, to learn, to try to understand a different person. It can be shallow and fragile if it is lived on the surface, denying or pushing aside the unpleasantness of life; it can lead to a deepening union when both persons are honest in facing the realities in their life together.

Experience and wisdom also make it clear to us that relationships do not survive the isolation of self-centeredness. Love means self-gift. The ideal of marriage says that spouse and family come before everything else: burying oneself in work, obsessive ambition for advancement, desire to accumulate great wealth, coveted time for personal leisure. A marriage requires in the part of both persons to identify and seek out the ways of living that provide stability, respect and peace—that develop the generosity and patience of a true friendship. When he accepted greater responsibility at work, Bill had to balance the new commitment with time to be with Susan during difficult medical procedures; with time to take Chris to visit a number of high schools as he came to his important decision; with time to celebrate Jill's triumphs in swimming competitions.

And the family unit cannot turn in on itself, but needs to reach out, to give to others. In the midst of its own concerns, the family can put aside time on a regular basis to serve at a nearby soup kitchen; to do chores and run errands for an elderly couple on their block. This thoughtfulness for the welfare of others is a source of deeper union for the whole family.

In reflecting on experience, we come to realize that suffering need not be destructive but can in fact bring new depth to love. The Scriptures tell us that Christ was made perfect through suffering. The experience of Bill and Susan sees the forging of their union in the trials and difficulties confronting them. Indeed, suffering has a way of making us like children: more spontaneous in loving, more willing to risk everything, with fewer restrictions on our hopes. The more drastic the trial, the clearer our priorities become. It is the little everyday annoyances that need our more constant attention. A friendship, a marriage, is seldom destroyed with a single blow; more likely it is by a gradual eating away at the roots. Self-gift is the lifesource; self-sufficiency and self-centeredness are the fatal disease. The ideal of human love is indeed attractive: "This is why a man leaves his father and mother and clings to his wife;" it is also demanding: "They are no longer two, therefore, but one body."

THE RISKS OF MARRIAGE

by Sean Freeman

DIVORCE is very much a part of modern life—even for Catholics. The figures keep climbing. Almost one out of three marriages ends in divorce, the statisticians tell us. And those who divorce and remarry face even worse odds the second time around. But aside from reiterating Jesus' unequivocal words against it, there's very little any sermonizer can say that will affect either the appalling statistics or modify the words of Jesus.

What we can reflect upon to some advantage, perhaps, is marriage itself—a living, delicate, intimate, rewarding, demanding, always complex, sometimes trying relationship between a woman and a man. Marriage has never been a perfect institution because it is really not susceptible to being institutionalized. There are those theologians who now freely admit that the church has been wrong to view it as an institution and to treat it like an organization or club which has a set charter, laws of operation, ground rules, and the like. They say that the church really should not have become so deeply involved in the "marriage business."

And it is true that for many centuries Christians did not get married in the church—literally. They married each other in private or small family settings. After more centuries it became the custom to invite a priest to come by after the ceremony to bless the new couple. And, at length, and quite possibly to spare the priest a long walk in bad weather, people began to get married in church after a Mass had been said as the blessing. It was never true, nor is it true today, that the church or the priest marries a couple. They marry each other.

What the church and the priest can do is remind the couple of Jesus' words, pray with the couple that they will have the grace and strength to heed those words for a lifetime, instruct the couple in the church's teachings about the morality of reproduction and the sacredness of life, and remind them that their union is a reflection of Christ's own intimate union with and love for the church—the people of God.

A good marriage makes its own rules, and all marriages carry grave responsibilities on the part of one spouse for the other, and for both with regard to any children they may have. In these matters they are answerable to God; and in certain matters of financial support and property they are answerable to courts of law should they decide to separate. The church has made its own set of laws governing marriage and divorce, as well.

But all the laws in the world cannot sustain a loving relationship, and that is what marriage really is. Only the two people involved can do that and they do well to ask God in prayer for all the help they can get. Most of all, they must firmly resolve to make of their relationship a perfect microcosm embodying the two great commandments of

Themes from the Bible

Jesus—to love God, and to love each other as they love themselves. If there is no patience in marriage, where will there be patience? If there is no forgiveness, no tolerance, no thoughtfulness between wife and husband, where will it be in their lives? If married people cannot "die to themselves" for the sake of the other, if they do not seek to serve, to minister, to please, to praise—to love—where else in their lives will they do so? And these are the basics of the Christian life.

A good marriage is truly a reflection of the relationship between Christ and his church—church in the sense of all those who follow him. In the heart of our families we learn how to be Christians; if parents want to make their children Christians, then their example—the unarticulated example of a relationship which is selfless—is the most potent teaching and conversion force there is.

These are lofty sentiments, to be sure. If they were followed, there should never be a separation or a divorce. But the facts, the statistics make it plain that this is not the case. Why? Sociologist Andrew Greeley sums up some of the reasons: "The community support that helps to hold a marital relationship together is not as strong as it used to be. Husbands and wives spend relatively little time together compared to what they used to spend in the old peasant villages. The legal and social structures of society no longer constrain a married couple to maintain appearances of unity even when all affection is gone. Finally, in the post-Freudian era we expect much more out of human intimacy that we did in years gone by. A clean house, well-dressed children, a paycheck at the right time, good appearances in society—there was once a time when this was all that one could reasonably expect from a marriage. Now we also expect self-fulfillment, personality development, a challenge, satisfaction, play and a perpetual love affair. Contemporary marriages break up more often because contemporary expectations from marriage are much higher."

But, as Father Greeley goes on to point out, there is really nothing wrong with such increased expectations. There is nothing un-Christian about them. In fact they are actually deeply Christian in their reflection of a desire for a more fulfilling life and a rejection of sham and hypocrisy. The fact is that modern Christian marriage is a greater challenge than it has ever been—but that is no reason to fear it. For what it challenges is our commitment to the Christian life. It is far easier to drift along and stay together for appearance's sake than it is to work hard, and pray hard, at making our new and richer relationships in marriage work—work and reflect the love of Jesus in our lives.

Greater expectations in marriage call for greater commitment. This means that marriage is not to be undertaken lightly. It is no longer enough—it never really was—to go blindly into such an intimate, profoundly central relationship. If we only "expect" things from marriage without also expecting to give of ourselves and of our love with no thought of "keeping things even," without wanting to give everything we have simply because we want to give it the one we love, then we run a personal and a Christian risk. For, just as it is true that no one but the two lovers has the power to marry them but themselves, it is equally true that no one except themselves has the power to separate them and destroy this unity of persons. Jesus' words then apply not to divorce courts or tribunals, but directly to the married couple: "What God has joined together, let no man [or woman] divide."

FAIL AT LOVE, FAIL AT LIFE

by Paul J. Wadell

A PERSONAL story from my own family may bring to
the homilist's or congregation's memory similar stories
of one's own. Not long ago I received a letter from my
sister, Anne. The letter was written shortly after the four-
teenth anniversary of our grandmother's death. In that letter Anne reflected on the special person our grandmother
was, and called her a saint. She knew that our grandmother, whom we affectionately called MeMa, was not
well-educated; she knew that her life, according to most
standards, was not vastly successful, and she knew that
when MeMa died no monuments would be erected in her
name. Still, fourteen years after her death she was vividly
present in a memory; fourteen years after her death here
was my sister calling her, a woman the world hardly knew,
a saint. Why?

Perhaps because my grandmother was eminently successful at the one thing that matters: love. She needs no
monuments by which to remember her, for we who were
so unfailingly loved by her remember her life as a monu-
ment to love.

When Anne wrote that letter she recalled an event. It
happened on a Sunday evening when Anne was nineteen,

Themes from the Bible

a time in her life when, as she put it, "I was confused about who I was or who I wanted to be. I was moody, up and down a lot, and not always the easiest person to get along with. But MeMa didn't care." On this Sunday evening Anne was in the kitchen, standing with her plate, waiting to dish out food for dinner. MeMa was behind her. Then something happened. "I felt her put her arms around me from behind," Anne recalled, "and lay her head against my back and give me a quiet hug. She felt so tiny and frail and I suddenly realized that she would not be with us forever. But at that moment I also knew how much I loved her. She knew all about me and yet she still could embrace me and love me. I know I will never be as good as MeMa....We were so lucky to have known her."

There could not have been a more perfect deed. In one sense, my grandmother's act seems so slight, so inconsequential, a wordless touch, a momentary embrace. But it was not a trivial event. There was power in that touch, there was life in it; one woman's touch kept another woman alive. A miracle took place that Sunday evening, for in my grandmother's love God broke more fully into our world. Through an act of such unadorned goodness, the world inched closer to fullness.

Fourteen years later that deed endures, still giving life to Anne, maybe giving life to those who will hear this story. My grandmother knew how to do for Anne exactly what Anne needed, she was a genius at that, and I think I know why. MeMa had spent a lifetime loving God.

Although we are familiar with the gospel command to love, it is easy to become lackadaisical about this, to dismiss it as something we already know, to tune out what may have become a tired, worn message; but that would be a dangerous move. After all, to have failed at love is to have failed at life; that is the message that lingers.

To ask "Which is the greatest commandment?" is to ask, "What is the most life-giving thing we can do?" To pose this question is to inquire into the kind of behavior that captures best what a human being is. There are many things we do, many things we do quite well, but there is one thing supreme we are called to master, and that is love. To love God and neighbor is the bedrock requirement of our lives; unless we practice love we cannot have life at all; to neglect it is to waste ourselves.

But love also brings likeness. The plot of the Christian life is to make our way back to God. That signifies not so much a change of place but of person. Something has to happen to us through life, there is a change we must undergo, a transformation we must suffer. To be human is to realize we are not yet who we should be or need to be; rather, we are, at best, only partially ourselves, stuttering reminders of a promise yet unfulfilled. That promise is captured in the kingdom, but the kingdom describes not a place, but a relationship we have with God when we have become enough like God to find joy, happiness, and peace in him. How do we attain such likeness? By loving God wholeheartedly, passionately, completely. We are commanded to love God most of all because every love brings likeness to whatever is loved, and loving God brings the likeness requisite for wholeness, the likeness requisite for peace. We make our way back to God through wholehearted love for God.

A scene in Walker Percy's novel *The Second Coming* captures this. The depressed hero of the book, Will Barrett, a man out-of-sorts, reflects that no one is "a hundred per cent themselves" anymore. "More likely they were forty-seven per cent themselves. . . . All too often these days they were two per cent themselves, specters who hardly occupied a place at all." The question then is "how to restore the ninety-eight per cent?"

The answer, of course, is love. Human beings are creatures of devotion. In order to live we must live for something more, we must seek something higher than ourselves, because for some strange reason we find the center of ourselves outside ourselves. This is what it means to love, to expend oneself for something inestimably good. If we are only two per cent ourselves, it is because we have not found the life that comes through love. If we are mere ghosts of ourselves, mere slivers of fullness, maybe it is because we have not yet realized how selfishness shrivels us and generosity makes us whole. To be selfish, isolated, enclosed is not to protect the self, it is to act against the self. We are not naturally selfish, we are sinfully selfish. What we naturally are is lovers, people who seek the completion of themselves outside themselves, people who sense that fullness of life comes not in isolation but communion.

That is how the missing ninety-eight per cent is restored, through a love which seeks others. It is restored most of all in a wholehearted love for God because friendship with God offers life in a way nothing else can. In this Gospel, Jesus commands love not to burden us, but to show us where genuine freedom and fullness of life reside.

We cannot claim to love God if we live contrary to the

goodness of God. Paul speaks of this when he praises the Thessalonians as a faith community from whom "the word of the Lord has echoed forth . . . resoundingly." Paul is saying that people have come to know God and experience God through the love and goodness of the Thessalonians. He explains what Anne felt that evening. God is present through people who love; God gets spoken through kindness.

Not to love God wholeheartedly diminishes the self. Human beings are creatures of devotion, but if we are not foremost devoted to God we undertake a way of life which is essentially diminishing. One practical task would be to examine the loves and attachments of our lives. Are we centered on God? Or have we become idolaters, people who love good things in the wrong way, people who have let other things have the place only God should have?

But it is not a love restricted to God. Any claim of love for God that does not work through love of neighbor is an empty boast. Are we people like the Thessalonians, those people through whom the Word of God resoundingly echoed forth?

NO RESTRICTIONS ON THE
LAW OF LOVE

by Henry Fehrenbacher

ONE day a priest was walking down the broken, lit-tered streets in the slum area of a big city. He was depressed as he looked around, for here and there he had to be careful not to stumble over the bodies of derelicts who were asleep or who had passed out. Others who were shuffling by or just loitering were unshaven and grimy, in tattered clothes, and had vacuous looks in their eyes. The buildings were as delapidated as the people, and any deepset doorway smelled of urine. The air was hot, heavy, humid. No breeze stirred.

Sitting on one doorstep was a forlorn shape, the epitome of despair and hopelessness. It was a man whose wrinkled face barely showed through a week's beard; his hands were dirty, his black, ragged pants, ill-fitting, and on his feet, to which some battered sandals barely clung, there were no socks.

Then the priest noticed another abject figure approach-ing; he, too, had matted, greasy hair and grimy clothes. Another one of the lost souls of this world, thought the priest. The man was swigging beer from a bottle wrapped in a brown paper bag. But this man, seeing the forlorn figure on the steps, paused long enough to hand him the unfinished bottle of beer. It was done quietly, without a word. A look of surprise brightened the recipient's face, gratitude showed in his glazed eyes, and he put the bottle to his mouth.

The priest's eyes brightened also and his soul was lifted from depression, for in this brief and fleeting incident he saw the presence of Christ. The priest had seen an act of love, an act of grace, an act of Jesus Christ. Jesus had promised to be with us until the end of time, and he was here in this moment of compassion.

"God is Love," wrote St. John (1 John 4:8), and Jesus is the image of his Father. Here is the church, thought the priest, for where Christ is, there is the church. We can make a thousand laws and regulations, we can decree a thousand rubrics for ritual, and we can declare a thousand dogmas, but without love we do not have a church, for love is the essence of God, the basis of our faith, the necessary element which binds us to God and to each other.

Our religion must come from our heart. Although most of the Pharisees were good people, Jesus pointed out that for some of them external observance was the main ingredient of their religion, and they used this to enhance their own public positions. They widened their phylacteries, wore huge tassels, sought out places of honor at banquets and front seats in the synagogues, and loved titles.

On another occasion Jesus accused them of cleansing the outside of the cup, according to ritual laws, but of being filled with rapaciousness and evil within. If you want to be wiped clean, he said, give what you have as alms. You pay tithes on insignificant herbs, he told them, "while neglecting justice and the love of God" (Luke 11:37-44).

Through the prophet Malachi God protested that people were not keeping his ways, but were showing partiality in their decisions. Paul was happy that the Thessalonians accepted his preaching as God's message, not as the word of men. True greatness, says Jesus, comes from serving others, for that is the expression of the love of God and neighbor.

Jesus was not objecting to teachers and fathers but to people who merely wanted those honorific titles without teaching the message of Jesus or without being fatherly as God is. Surface piety is not acceptable. All societies, including our religious society, the church, need form and structure and some rules and regulations so that we may function more easily together, but these must not become the object of our religion.

This is why the Second Vatican Council attempted to simplify things. When Catholics got to be known as the people who didn't eat meat on Friday rather than the people who love each other (John 13:35), we knew that something was amiss, and Pope John XXIII called the council. The temptation to be satisfied by or to think oneself meritorious by superficial observance was obviously not limited to the scribes and Pharisees and other people of Jesus' time; it is an ever-present temptation.

Jesus was angry when the Pharisees were watching to see if he would heal the man with a shriveled hand on the Sabbath. In their mind, to heal on the Sabbath would be against the rules. They did not have compassion for the man; they only wanted to catch Jesus breaking a religious regulation. This followed their complaint that the disciples on the Sabbath were picking corn to eat. "The Sabbath was made for man," Jesus told them, "not man for the Sabbath" (Mark 2:23-3:1-5).

Perhaps so many Catholics have left the church in the past twenty-five years or so because they only saw the structure or the form, not the substance. Their vision of Christ was obstructed by the phylacteries and tassels and titles, as it were. A religious discussion is not an analysis of church rules and regulations; rather, it is an exploration of the good news of Jesus Christ. Man-made strictures must not keep us from the love and compassion of Jesus. We must not put limitations on Jesus or organize him into sterility.

"Have we not all the one Father?" asks Malachi. When we realize that we have the same Father as Jesus we need no other title or honor. Herein lies true humility. As brothers and sisters of Jesus we want to be like him, so love and compassion come first. This is the heart of our religion.

"The church of the diaspora (our times), if it is to remain alive at all," wrote theologian Karl Rahner, "will be a church of active members, a church of the laity; a laity conscious of itself as bearing the church in itself, as constituting her, and not being simply an object for her—i.e., the clergy—to look after."

We need not look for honors and titles, for we can have no greater honor than to have God for our Father; we need no other title than being called sons and daughters of our heavenly Father. We need no other religious structure than being the family of God. And we need no other rule or

Themes from the Bible

law or regulation than the great law of both the Old and the New Testament, love of God and neighbor. And we need no larger tassels or wider phylacteries; we need only to clothe ourselves in Christ (Galatians 3:27), to be clothed in "sincere compassion, gentleness, patience and love" (Colossians 3:12).

THE DIVINE EMBRACE

by Daniel E. Pilarczyk

OVER the past few years medical science has learned an interesting thing about the care of infants. It seems that with even the best hospital treatment, sick infants recover better and faster if they get regular signs of human affection. In neonatal wards, there are staff persons who come around with some regularity and pick up the babies and cuddle them, and hug them, and talk to them. Then they put them back into their cribs. Statistically, those infants who receive this little bit of extra attention have a better chance of recovery than those who do not. Probably the babies don't know or recognize who is making this little fuss over them, but at least they realize somehow that someone cares, that someone loves them. And for many, this makes the difference between survival and death.

In a way we are all like that. We need to know that somebody loves us, that somebody cares; otherwise we tend to shrivel up. We may not die physically, but our life can seem to come to an end inside of us simply because there just doesn't seem to be any reason to keep on going.

Liturgically, Christmas is not the biggest feast of the church's year. Easter is. The reason is that Christmas marks only the beginning of our salvation by Jesus, a salvation that is brought to its completion through the totality of his life, and especially through his death and resurrection. Moreover, in some parts of the church, the celebration of the birth of Christ is overshadowed by the celebration of his manifestation to the Magi and to the world in the epiphany. But there is something special about Christmas, and that something special is that in being born as a human being, God shows that he loves us enough to want to be with us, to want to be one of us. Christmas is one of the wordless ways in which God hugs us, embraces us with his love.

Of course God's love for his human creatures is not something that began with the birth of Jesus. It is something that had gone on for a long time. This is the significance of the passages from Isaiah where he talks about the ways in which God comforted his people Israel in the past and would comfort them again in the future. Isaiah shows us a God who puts caring arms around us and says, "Don't cry. Everything is going to be all right."

The Gospel indicates that God's becoming a human being in Jesus is not something he decided to do on the spur of the moment. No, it was carefully planned from all eternity and arranged in such a way that the events of secular history—Caesar Augustus, a census, the need to travel to a different town—conspired to bring about what God had in mind and bring it about in a way that was in accord with his purposes.

God's word reminds us that the birth of Christ at Bethlehem is only the beginning of the execution of God's plan. There is more still to come, a more which includes

LET THERE BE LOVE

the universal lordship of Jesus over all creation, in company with those he has made his own.

What we see here is that the birth of Christ is only one moment in God's careful scheme of love for us, a scheme that stretches from the most intimate levels of God's own life till the very end of time. God is not one who loves impulsively, or who loves and then walks away. God is an eternal lover.

And yet, Christmas is a special moment in the eternal scheme of God's love for us, and its specialness may lie in its simplicity. A child is born in a cave, away from home, unpretentious, poor. To be sure, there were signs that this child was not just another human baby. Angels announced his birth to the shepherds, and later the Magi would come. But the basic fact remains that this was a human baby, a baby who was there just because God wanted to be with his human creatures, just because God wanted to be with *us*. The birth of Jesus on this silent night is a silent sign of God's affection, a quiet indication that we are important to our divine Lord.

Notice, though, that it's not because of anything *we* have done that we are important to God. It's not that we have deserved or earned his coming to us. It's not a matter of our individual worth or our personal achievements. It's not that we have some claim to be related to God in our humanity. We are important to him simply because he has chosen to create human persons, simply because he has chosen to love us, apart from any consideration of merit on our part. He loves us—and he loves us all—just because that's the way he is. And that's what God is trying to tell

us—simply and straightforwardly—on this feast of Jesus'
birth in our midst.

Perhaps the most practical thing we could take away
from the eucharistic celebration of the birth of Jesus is a
remembrance of who we are. We are lots of different
things, of course. We are fathers and mothers. We are children and teenagers. We are blue-collar workers and doctors and accountants. Some who are here today have ter-
minal illnesses and fear that they may never celebrate
another Christmas. Some are alcoholics. Some are struggling with family problems and sex problems and job problems and church problems. Some haven't felt the need to
celebrate with our community since last Christmas. Some
are lonely. Some are on the brink of despair. Some see
themselves as just ordinary people who are trying to live
up to their responsibilities one day at a time, wondering,
sometimes, whether their life means anything.

But all of us have one thing in common. All of us share
one basic reality that puts everything else into perspective.
And that is that we are loved by God, loved enough that
he has chosen to become like us and live among us. That's
what we are. That's who we are. And that's pretty good.
It might be useful for each of us to say to ourselves at some
point in this Christmas liturgy, "I am Mary Smith or John
Doe. My life is. . .whatever it is. And God loves me. And
God has told me that he loves me by being with me, by
being like me."

But we can't stop with *me*. We must also say, "God is
like me, but he is like everybody around me in this church
and this world as well. God is like the poor and the home-

less, the persecuted and the derelict. God is like the people I love and like the people I can't stand. And he has chosen to be like them for the same reason he has chosen to be like me: just because he loves."

So the second thing we must to say to ourselves as we celebrate Christmas is, "Lord, if I am like you because you are like me, help me to reach out to help and understand and acknowledge and forgive and love all those for whom this day is intended to be a sign of your affection. Help me to reach out to them as you have reached out to me."

We started this Christmas reflection by talking about babies and cribs and hugging and making a fuss. We talked about the human need for attention and affection. It ought to be clear by now that *we* are the infants, that *we* are the ones who need to be hugged and reassured, all of us. And the one who picks us up and puts his arms around us and reassures us is none other than the Lord himself. That's what we celebrate at Christmas.

THE HOME OF THE HEART

by Marcella Hermesdorf

IN his *Living the Vows*, Robert J. McAllister describes a family in which the mother's quest to live a "spiritual" life, to be a good Christian by giving unselfish service to her parish and community, ironically undermines her own family life. It seems that she spent so much time attending retreats and workshops, volunteering for parish activities and committees, and helping various priests and sisters in her community with their ministries, that she had little left to give her own family. Consequently, her husband described their marriage as a "farce and a failure," and her children said they felt "neglected and unloved."

The situation described is just one example of Christian family life gone sour because of misplaced values. In this case, the values are obviously sound—giving and serving—but they are *not* practiced where they should be—in the home. Friends, acquaintances, and strangers receive the care, love, and compassion which should be showered on the woman's family.

Sometimes values are misplaced in other ways. Material goods and well-being are substituted, consciously or unconsciously, for love and affection, care and support. For example, a father spends so much time on his job(s) making money to buy just one more convenience for his wife, one more gift for his son or daughter, that his family rarely sees him, much less spends time with him. He believes the material goods reflect his love; his family just wishes he were home long enough to talk to them, play with them, to give and receive a loving touch or a comforting embrace.

In his letter to the Colossians, Paul talks of their relationships to one another and their relationship to their God. He reminds his listeners that they are, by reason of their baptisms, "chosen," "holy," and "beloved." Because they are beloved, they must love, must treat one another with kindness and compassion, patience, and "heartfelt"—interior—mercy. Because they are forgiven, they must forgive one another. Because the Word dwells in them, they are to speak words of instruction and admonishment to one another and words of thanksgiving and praise to God. Paul makes us look beneath virtuous acts to the attitudes that underlie them.

Paul speaks specifically to family members. Reminding them that they are now "in the Lord," he asks wives to be submissive to their husbands, husbands to love their wives, and children to be obedient to their parents. Though twentieth-century hearers may bristle at Paul's advice to wives, we must remember that Paul was not making unusual demands for his time. All good Jewish men, women, and children knew how they were to behave with family members. But Paul takes his hearers beyond behavior to attitude. Ordinary familial duties motivated by obedience to the Law become actions performed out of love. Paul's exhortations are based on his belief in the "conversion" of

Themes from the Bible

hearts. From "I must" or "I should" to "I want to." From a sense of mere obligation to a deep desire of loving service.

Though we have little information about the relationships between Mary, Joseph, and Jesus, Luke's Gospel suggests what their family life together must have been like. First of all, Mary and Joseph are faithful to the Law, presenting themselves at the temple at the prescribed time—to offer sacrifice, to present their first-born son, to have Mary undergo the rites of purification. When Jesus was older, they would take him to Jerusalem for the feast of Passover. As parents, they obeyed the Law of the Lord and raised their Son according to its dictates.

But Jesus' later life also suggests that Mary and Joseph lived according to the Spirit of the Law. His behavior to the poor and sick, to children, to widows, to Peter's mother-in-law reflects love, compassion, mercy, and kindness—all the attitudes spoken of by Paul. Jesus must have learned these attitudes from his parents. For though much has changed in the last two thousands years, the fact that men and women learn and behave according to the values which pervade their homes has certainly *not* changed. Jesus' loving actions are a result not only of his divine nature but of his human upbringing as well.

Another attitude Jesus seems to have learned was respect for women. We surmise that Joseph treated Mary with great respect and love. How else can we account for Jesus' love for Martha and Mary, for his compassion and forgiveness of the adultress, for his respectful treatment of the Samaritan woman?

LET THERE BE LOVE

Jesus' view of authority likewise must have resulted from his experiences of parental authority. Mary and Joseph must have exercised their authority lovingly and gently. How else do we account for Jesus' teaching that one in authority must be ready to serve all? The values Jesus preached and lived must have existed in his own home.

Just as we can imagine what characterized the relationships among Mary, Joseph, and Jesus because of Jesus' behavior as an adult, so we can speculate on his attitude and behavior toward his parents based on his treatment of others. We *do* know that he loved his mother enough to provide an adopted son for her as he faced death. He must have treated her with similar compassion and mercy throughout his early life, though it is true that, like all children, he needed eventually to exercise his independence of her as well—in the temple at Cana when he was twelve.

For her part, Mary had to "let go" of her child at the proper moment. Simeon's words to her today refer, of course, to the sorrows she would suffer because she was the mother of the Messiah. But the sorrow Simeon speaks of is applicable to all parents, who must eventually allow their children to make their own choices, sometimes to make their own mistakes. Career and vocation choices are often beyond the understanding or approval of one's parents. But it is a parent's lot to "let go"—painful as that may be.

Jesus' relationshp with his mother is certainly described in more detail than his relationship with Joseph. But if Jesus treated his mother tenderly, he must have respected and

Themes from the Bible

loved Joseph as well. Though the scriptures are silent on this issue, a Jesus reared in the Spirit and Letter of the Law must have revered his human father. Jesus probably cared for him gently as he aged, according to the teachings of Sirach. It is likely that Jesus was present at Joseph's death-bed, a source of comfort for both his mother and his father. Hidden as Jesus' early life was, surely the household must have been filled with the love, consideration, and kindness which underlies the Law-prescribed duties of family members to one another. Why else would Jesus have remained at home for thirty years? It could not have been easy for him to leave such a home.

The Holy Family, then, not only acted toward one another as the Law demanded, they were prompted by the Spirit underlying the Law. Love, mercy, kindness, respect, and honor resided in their Nazareth home.

How different the home of the Holy Family from that of the aforementioned "workaholic" father and of the over-committed mother. The father has been so busy providing material goods, he hasn't been at home long enough to love and honor his wife, to provide guidance and give affection to his children. Material values have replaced spiritual ones. The over-committed mother, on the other hand, has maintained the proper values; she has just forgotten that "charity begins at home."

Let us ask ourselves how we behave toward our parents, our spouses, our children. Are we with them long enough to interact with them at all? And, if we do spend time with them, do we merely perform empty duties? Or do we act lovingly, as befits sons and daughters of a loving God,

144

descendants in faith of Sirach and Paul? Would someone observing our family life see in it a reflection of the family life in Nazareth?

Let us ask God for continual conversion of heart that we might treat the members of our family with the same reverance and compassion, love and respect that filled the lives of Joseph, Mary, and Jesus.

THE VOCATION OF FAMILY

by Henry Fehrenbacher

IN family life, we are sensitive to each other's needs. We quietly and lovingly take care of each other. We need each other and we need each other's love. God had brought us together so that we can help each other and receive from each other. Family life is a vocation, a calling from God, and we must answer to God for our family life. At ten o'clock every night on a New York TV station an announcer says, "It is ten o'clock. Parents, do you know where your children are?" It is similar to the questions that God will ask on judgment day, "Where are your children? Where is your husband? Where is your wife?" And God might well ask children, "Where are your parents?"

For both children and parents make up a family. So the children also have a responsibility for the success and happiness of a famiy. We hope that the days of blaming only the parents for failures in the family are over. Even single people and those whose wives or husbands have died are still somewhat responsible for family life, for they are still related to families and can be of help to families.

Although the gospel writers did not find it necessary or useful to tell us much about the domestic life of Jesus, Mary, and Joseph, a feast celebrating the Holy Family was attached to the liturgical calendar in 1921—it is a very recent feast. There were feasts of Jesus, Mary, and Joseph separately, but now we celebrate their life together in Nazareth. It was a holy family because each of the members was holy. Perhaps because the family, long considered the basis of society, was falling on hard times, church authorities established the feast to show that we should not be saints in isolation but that we must be saints as social beings.

We would never have heard of Mary and Joseph if it had not been for Jesus. They are important because of their relationship to him. Our family life also is based on a relationship to God or it means nothing. Mary accepted the motherhood of Jesus because it was God's will. "Be it done to me according to thy word." An angel of God explains to Joseph the position of Mary, and Joseph becomes the foster-father of Jesus because it is God's will. Joseph takes the child and Mary to Egypt because it is God's will. As was customary at the time, Joseph was the head of the family. He was, says Matthew, an upright man, a man of honor, who, before the explanation by the angel, was unwilling to expose Mary to the law and wanted to spare her publicity.

Their home was probably just one room, with maybe extra space for a small kitchen or for storage, made of stone or mud bricks, with a clay floor partly covered with rush mats. The interior was dark and the roof was leaky. There was no running water and no privacy. Joseph and Jesus had blue collar jobs—they were both carpenters.

Members of a family should not love each other less

because of their faults. The worse the father, mother, wife, husband, or child is the more that person needs the love of the others. In family life, says Paul, we need mercy, kindness, humility, meekness, patience, and forgiveness, but above all we must love. His litany of family virtues would make a good examination of conscience for us each night as we say our night prayers.

It is not absolutely true that the family that prays together stays together, for saintly parents can have wayward children and saintly children can have sinful parents, but a home will not be a Christian home without prayer. Prayer together is certainly good for a family, for the family then sees its calling from God to be a family. It is sad that even the custom of prayer at meals is falling into disuse.

"Let the word of Christ, rich as it is," says Paul, "dwell in you." There are families where the Bible is read, even briefly, each day by the family together. Such families are guided and bonded together by the word of God. Family religious customs must be set by the parents and kept up no matter how difficult. Children desperately need parents of strong faith. And the children cannot be fooled; they can see the faith of the parents.

The fourth commandment does not say, "Children, obey your parents." It tells children to honor their parents. This is greater than mere obedience. We don't like the word obedience, but we all obey in many ways all of our lifetime. We obey a multitude of laws and customs. The book of Sirach speaks of honoring our parents, but there must be authority in the home. So Paul says, "Children, obey your

parents in everything as the acceptable way in the Lord."
Jesus, although he was the Son of God, obeyed Mary and
Joseph. And he obeyed his heavenly Father. Parents must
make themselves worthy of honor and obedience. And
parents who do not demand obedience are cheating their
children.

Family life does not end when the children get married
or are old enough to leave home. The child-parent relationship is always there. We hear of "throw-away" children
these days, but we also hear of many lonely old people
whose children do not visit them. The prophet Sirach tells
us to take care of our parents when they are old. We should
also read the book of Tobit. It is a beautiful account of
family life. "When I die," the father Tobit tells his son
Tobias, "give me a decent burial. Honor your mother and
do not abandon her as long as she lives. Do whatever
pleases her and do not grieve her spirit in any way.
Remember, my son, that she went through many trials for
your sake while you were in her womb."

Children, do not give up on your parents. They need
your love and help. Remember that neither did Joseph and
Mary understand Jesus when they found him in the temple. Parents, do not give up on your children. Remember
St. Monica, whose son was a great sinner. Her love and
prayers for him never ceased, and he became a great saint.

Many people today—and in the past—have taken family
ties for granted. And it's natural that we don't spend our
every waking hour examining relationships which rise up
so naturally and which pervade our lives in so many sub-
liminal ways. While it's true that not all families are filled

with sweetness and light, it is the rare one in which love, however silently expressed, does not exist in some form. Today it might help to think about the various ways that our family has loved and supported us, and examine our response to that love. Do we take it for granted? If so how, at least once, can we show each member of our family that we appreciate and reciprocate that love. Tomorrow may be too late.

CONTRIBUTORS

KATHLEEN CANNON, a Dominican Sister, is an Assistant Professor of Homiletics at the Catholic Theological Union in Chicago. She is a frequent contributor to pastoral and homiletic publications.

JAMES A. CONNOR is a Jesuit priest who has taught English at Gonzaga University and is well known for his essays and short stories. His works have appeared in *The Critic, Willow Run* and *New Catholic World*. A collection of his fiction, *God's Breath and Other Stories*, has been critically acclaimed.

ANDREW COSTELLO has served as Novice Master for the Redemptorists of the Baltimore Province at their Mt. St. Alphonsus novitiate in Esopus, New York. Among his very popular books are *Thank God It's Friday: Meditations for Hardworking Catholics, Cries But Silent...* and *Listenings* (all published by the Thomas More Press).

HENRY FEHRENBACHER is best known for his stimulating column which has been featured in *U.S. Catholic* for more than 25 years. Father Fehrenbacher, a native of Minnesota, has served as pastor in a number of small Minnesota towns and has visited more than 60 countries in his travels.

151

Themes from the Bible

TIMOTHY FITZGERALD has postgraduate degrees in theology from the University of Louvain and in liturgy from the University of Notre Dame. Father Fitzgerald has served as Associate Pastor of Our Lady's Immaculate Heart Church in Ankeny, Iowa, is the author of *Confirmation: A Parish Celebration*, and is a frequent contributor to liturgical publications.

SEAN FREEMAN is author of *The Thomas More Bible Prayerbook* and *Parables, Psalms and Prayers* (Thomas More Press). His insightful articles appear frequently in *The Critic*. He is a magna cum laude graduate of Notre Dame.

NORBERT F. GAUGHAN is the Bishop of Gary, Indiana. Formerly a priest of the Diocese of Pittsburgh and Auxiliary Bishop of Greensburg, Pennsylvania, he earned his Ph.D. from the University of Pittsburgh. He has taught philosophy at the University of Pittsburgh-Greensburg; is an accomplished photographer; writes a provocative weekly column; and is the author of the highly-praised *Troubled Catholics: The Lessons of Discontent*.

ANDREW M. GREELEY, a priest of the Archdiocese of Chicago, is a sociologist, a critic, a novelist, and a commentator on the contemporary scene. Multi-talented, he has published more than a hundred books ranging from sociological treatises to best-selling novels. His most recent is *God in Popular Culture* (Thomas More Press).

LET THERE BE LOVE

MARCELLA HERMESDORF, a Sinsinawa Dominican, teaches English at Rosary College, River Forest, Illinois, where she is also an advisor to foreign students. She formerly served as director of Rosary's London Program as well as its campus ministry.

WILLIAM A. HERR received his Ph.D. from the Institut Superieur de Philosophie of the University of Louvain and is the author of *This Our Church* and *Catholic Thinkers in the Clear* as well as the forthcoming *In Search of Christian Wisdom* (Thomas More Press). He has taught Latin, philosophy, and psychology and now lives and works in Boston.

MARY PETER McGINTY is a member of the Congregation of St. Joseph and Associate Professor of Theology at Loyola University in Chicago. Sister Mary Peter, who received her Ph.D. from Marquette University, writes and lectures primarily on sacramental theology.

RAWLEY J. MYERS is a parish priest in Colorado Springs, Colorado, the author of many magazine articles and of eight books, the most recent of which is *Jesus is Here.* He has a doctorate in philosophy from Catholic University and was formerly editor of a diocesan newspaper, chaplain at the University of Nebraska, and a diocesan director of vocations.

Themes from the Bible

DANIEL E. PILARCZYK, Archbishop of the Cincinnati Archdiocese, was ordained a priest in 1959 and consecrated a bishop in 1974. He served as Auxiliary Bishop of Cincinnati until 1982 when he was appointed Archbishop. He was elected vice president of the National Conference of Catholic Bishops in 1936 and is a frequent contributor to the Catholic press.

PAUL J. WADELL is a member of the Passionist Community and served for two years in St. Louis, engaging in retreats and campus ministry. He returned to his doctoral studies at Notre Dame and received his doctorate in theology in 1985. He is Assistant Professor of Ethics at the Catholic Theological Union, Chicago.